SELECTED POEMS

Bertolt Brecht

TRANSLATION AND INTRODUCTION BY H. R. HAYS

Selected Poems

A Harvest Book

Harcourt Brace Jovanovich, Inc., New York

A B C D E F G H I J
ISBN 0-15-680646-0
Library of Congress Catalog Card Number 59-13887
Printed in the United States of America

ACKNOWLEDGMENT

The Introduction, "Brecht, Anti-Individualist," was previously published in *Poetry*.

Certain of these translations have appeared in *Poetry, Accent,* and *The Kenyon Review*.

CONTENTS

vii

INTRODUCTION

BRECHT, ANTI-INDIVIDUALIST

THE POETRY of Bertolt Brecht is representative of a tradition directly opposed to that which has been dominant in the United States in the period between two great wars. The afterflowering of Symbolism in English, coupled with movements which derived much of their inspiration from psychology, produced a highly individualistic art. The emphasis was all upon the uniqueness of the poet's sensitivity. Associative imagery replaced logic and ideas were presented with extreme indirectness. Perhaps the most novel contribution was the exploitation of sensation, a recording of the world in terms of a fantasy of the nerves. American poets of the twenties and thirties were, on the whole, nonpolitical. Even when they attempted social criticism they still worked in the tradition created by the Paris intellectuals. Most of such criticism took the form of personal malaise, dissatisfaction with ugliness and standardization or, more recently, anarchistic despair. This type of protest is also essentially individualistic. It stems from the ideal of the artist as a member of an elite, the conservator of sensitivity, good taste, and an honest outlook toward life. Despite minor reactions, individualism is typical of American poetry of the recent past, and it can be said that we have never had a school of political poetry.

Bertolt Brecht, a figure of great influence in German literature, has become the apostle of a reaction against individualism. His significance arises from the fact that his philosophy has molded his style and dictates the forms in which he works. In the editor's opinion he is almost the only social poet writing today, the only social poet whose form and matter coincide, the only political poet in the proper sense of the word.

It is scarcely necessary to stress the importance of Brecht's work at the present time. Now that nineteenth-century laissez-faire economy

3

has patently broken down, leaving doubt and confusion in its wake, all values are being challenged; and since automatically the state is encroaching more and more upon private life, the position of the individual is indeed perilous. Even our cultural individualism, dating from the Renaissance civilization, is on trial. While it would be hazardous to prophesy just what modification may take place in our concept of the individual, there is no doubt that contemporary thinking is in a state of flux. In consequence Brecht's repudiation of individual psychology, his rejection of Aristotelian tragedy, his attempt to go behind the Renaissance, and his interest in the formalism of Chinese drama, indicate that he is a precursor and a symptom of cultural revolution.

Brecht began writing when expressionism was dominant in Germany. His first book of verse, *Hauspostille*, published in 1927, is shot through with romantic bitterness and a kind of revolt through brutality. Himself a veteran of the first world war, he matured with a generation which had made the discovery that war was a tragic betrayal. His contemporaries were filled with a sense of the kinship of all peoples, a romantic, half-mystical hope for the future. Brecht reflects this wave of emotion but even in his earliest poems his skepticism is profound. There is a relation between this early poetry and the symbolo-surrealist poetry of France and other countries which followed the poetic leadership of Paris. The Rimbaudian note is struck in certain poems dealing with characters who have in common some quality of rebellion, either in terms of crime, bohemianism or adventurous challenging of nature. An impulse which in romance writing often led to humorous anarchy, in the work of the German poet appears as an intense preoccupation with the physically or morally unpleasant. There are many poems which deal with decay and death from an ambivalent attitude, a shifting from the philosophy of enjoy-the-moment to a toying with self-annihilation. The symbol of drowning appears again and again joined with an almost pleasurable interest in the gruesome. Whether this indicates a sensitivity to an underlying death wish in society or traditional German morbidity, it is clear that physical realism prepares us for another attitude which

4

dominates all of the poet's later work. For if the contemplation of misery, physical suffering, and death does not lead to mysticism or evasion, the natural alternative is a scrutiny of the causes for the horrors of existence: a writer who is essentially a materialist will seek for a materialist explanation. And in addition there was always in Brecht enough of the Protestant moralist and prophet to lead him back to the problem of human suffering.

The ballads, legendary fantasies and satirical grand guignol of this period were produced in a country which was quickly passing from a phase of revolutionary promise into a counter-revolution of inflation, profiteering and economic confusion that created a brutal contrast between the suffering masses and the bloated exploiters. Brecht looked about him and sensed that his world was rolling toward hell while those who profited from it rioted in cynical indifference.

The mood behind expressionism, as postwar realities grew grimmer and economic depression became world wide, was transformed. Translated into one type of action it led to still greater mysticism, fantasy and self-delusion—the hodge-podge ideology which was fascism. More realistic thinkers, digging into the causes of their disillusionment, sought for an economic explanation and many, including Brecht, embraced Marxist philosophy. Thus they had no choice but to relate their work to politics, and it is Brecht's great contribution that he made a serious attempt to marry literature and politics on a mature esthetic level.

By this time the left movement had made tremendous strides in Germany and the working class was the most politically developed and culturally advanced of any in Europe. This, in itself, was a tremendous stimulus to those artists who were seeking the answer to the social disintegration which they saw all about them. Brecht, like most left writers, felt the need for driving home certain facts, for telling the fundamental truths as he saw them. He abandoned all romanticism and ranged himself on the side of intellect, a position he has held to ever since. If, at times, it makes for dogmatism, his position is always clear. It followed, therefore, that the artist became a teacher,

5

a concept wholly opposed to that of the individualist, the member of an elite group. To the individualist, the subjective function of art, a concern with spiritual values, a sphere of consciousness closely related to the religious impulse, are all of the highest importance. For the poet of Brecht's school such elements are subordinated to a puritanical didacticism. This does not mean, however, that in matters of esthetic form he submits to group standards. In literary matters, like any specialist, he considers himself the best judge of what he is doing. What Brecht rebelled against was the anarchic morality of taste in the sphere of action and judgment. By taking a Marxist position, he was, like a Catholic writer of the Middle Ages, provided with a set of values to work with. He was like a teacher with a syllabus: the matter he wished to communicate was formulated, but his method of teaching remained his own.

In the twenties and thirties in Germany it looked as though the workers might soon seize power. Consequently social artists tried to abandon their class and place themselves at the service of the workers' movement. This movement, however, was sufficiently sophisticated from the cultural point of view so that Brecht's platform did not imply vulgarization. This is especially important for the American reader who is accustomed to considerable vague agitation for a "people's art." The familiar semi-Marxist in American letters, however, never clarifies his artistic problem. He is content to insert a plug for "progress" into a cliché formula. He generally fails to distinguish between folk art and art commercially popularized, and, at bottom, he is a sentimentalist. (For example, *Ballad for Americans*, which is remotely influenced by Brecht, is carried out on the Hollywood, radio, Tinpan Alley, commercialized folksy level.) In contrast Brecht was keenly aware of the dangers of muddled romanticism. He became the enemy of emotional self-indulgence to a fanatical degree. To counteract softness, impressionism and decorative lyricism, he attempted to create artistic forms out of didacticism itself. He discovered esthetic values in functionalism.

The philosophy of functional beauty is more familiar in the field of architecture and design than in literature. Architecture, being the most socially practical of the arts, has, in the modern period, responded to advances in technology and science to the extent of trying to erect an esthetic platform upon them. The consequent elimination of decoration and dependence upon forms automatically created by function and materials is the most recognizable characteristic of the international style. Constructivist sculpture, however, imitated the forms of modern architecture without the justification of function, and the painting of Piet Mondrian (which, it is claimed, in turn influenced architecture) represents a kind of conscious asceticism which certainly does not depend upon vulgar practicality but is rather what might be called classicism. In Germany some musicians also reacted against experimental modernism in favor of useful music (*Gebrauchsmusik*) and set about composing easily singable choral works and songs for the workers. All such symptoms indicate a trend antagonistic to romantic individualism, the trend of which Brecht is the literary representative. It is clear, however, from the above examples and also from Brecht's case, that there is a certain duality of purpose. While, in theory, Brecht is strictly practical, desirous of "spare speech, setting the words down cleanly," in order to teach a lesson, at the same time, as an artist, he is really seeking a classical style. And this is borne out by the fact that while his work is admired for its content, he has often had to face resistance to his forms among those politically sympathetic. All of which indicates that a genuine artist, whatever terms he makes with propagandistic aims, is always fundamentally interested in certain nonpractical values.

In the theater the result of Brecht's experiments has been controversial. The *Dreigroschenoper*, written during his more romantic period, made him famous all over Europe. His later works have produced angry arguments, even disturbances. The workers' audience has not always understood his subtleties and his bourgeois critics have been prejudiced against his point of view. Nevertheless he recreated a style of drama, developed the theory of the epic theater and, in this field, is distinctly a force to be reckoned with.

In lyric poetry circumstances united to make his task easier. It is clear that the only genuinely popular poetry is that which can be sung. The folk-song tradition is stronger in Germany and in German literature than in any other major section of European culture. Here was a form which was nonindividualist, a tool originally forged by the people, which could be resharpened and given back to them. Brecht from the beginning had worked in the ballad form and his subsequent political development merely called for a tempering process, the transformation of his verse into a battle cry, a marching song, a keener instrument for satire.

The language of the folk ballad is formalized and concrete. The older songs have touches of high style while the contemporary work song is full of shrewd satire and social protest. Except for William Blake, almost no poet in English has done much with the form. The nineteenth-century romantics imitated the metrical schemes and spoiled the language with abstractions and period clichés. Brecht, however, has successfully combined the elegance of the older imagery with the realistic bite of contemporary satire. That this requires great skill is proved by some of his imitators who fall into folksiness or mere doggerel.

What sustains Brecht is the dialectical basis of his philosophy and his sense of tradition. He does not grow maudlin over an abstract (and wholly fictitious) concept of the People, nor does he expose injustice as if discovering it for the first time. He assumes the existence of dialectical laws and plays on the resulting contradictions with bitter humor. His art is that of the fable, the modern morality play. At the same time his profound sensitivity to language and style impresses all German critics, regardless of ideology. He has borrowed from the sixteenth-century ballad, the nineteenth-century lied, the modern Tinpan Alley lyric—even Rudyard Kipling has had something to contribute. His genius for absorption is phenomenal and yet, at bottom, he is a traditional German poet still keeping alive the spirit of Heine. He is traditional in his essentially moral and philosophical temperament while his matter is wholly untraditional.

The poetry of Brecht's later period, collected in *Lieder, Gedichte*

8

Chöre, 1934, and *Svendborger Gedichte*, 1939, is therefore, in comparison with American verse, bare, austere, lacking in sensuous decoration. It depends for its effect upon sharpness of statement, epigrammatic contrast, uncompromising irony. The personal fantasy of the individualist has been completely eliminated. Images are used with economy, always dramatically, at the service of the idea. Only occasionally does a touch of latent romanticism emerge. The choruses from the play *Die Mutter*, and the anti-Nazi satires written for the radio, are examples of Brecht's most extreme functionalism. The choruses are deliberately primitive, a bare exposition of the dialectics of the action. With the additional emotive element of music they have a certain brutal strength. The very shock of their naked didacticism creates a theatrical effect. The satires approach nearer to journalism for they depend upon a knowledge of specific facts and events. Their esthetic element lies in the intellectual agility with which the poet plays on Marxist contradiction—a demolition through wit, analogous to the method of Pope. The ballads, both in and out of the dramas, mingle irony with emotional pathos. They are his most universally enjoyed poetic achievement. The device of expressing the most brutal and cynical precepts together with a melancholy reference to the ideal creates a specific poetic tension. *"Erst kommt das Fressen, dann kommt die Moral"* (First comes feeding, then morality) is the sentiment driven home again and again and always in angry, bitter or sad disillusionment. The cynically pathetic whore is one of his favorite characters, but she does not blame herself for her downfall, she puts the onus upon the audience. I am as you have made me, she says, and I can and will outdo you in ruthlessness. *"Denn für dieses Leben ist der Mensch nicht schlecht genug"* (For this world we live in none of us is bad enough). It is this tone of toughness and bitterness yet with sorrow behind it which expresses the pathos of humanity, the tragic unreality of idealism from the point of view of the dialectical materialist.

Brecht's cynicism has gone through a process of development and modification. When the sophisticated individualist decides that life is not what it might be, he is content to share his disillusionment with kindred emancipated souls in the belief that he has discovered an eternal verity. Brecht passes through this phase in his earlier work. *"Ihr sterbt mit allen Tieren und es kommt nichts nachher"* (You die like any beast, there's nothing after death) is a fairly familiar sentiment which generally leads to hedonistic irresponsibility. But as soon as he advances another step toward the social he arrives at an idealist-materialist contradiction. *"Die Welt ist arm, der Mensch ist schlecht. Wir wären gut—anstatt so roh, doch die Verhältnisse sie sind nicht so"* (The world is poor, man is bad. We would be good—instead of ruthless, but conditions don't permit us). From here he develops the frankly class point of view. Referring to the bourgeoisie, he says, *"Das Lateinisch ihrer bestochenen Pfaffen übersetze ich Wort für Wort in die gewöhnliche Sprache, da erweist es sich als Humbug"* (The Latin of their corrupt preachers I translate word for word into the vulgar tongue whereby it is revealed as humbug). The last statement is characteristic of his functional period in which he demonstrates the inevitable conflict between official morality and the fundamental drives of an acquisitive society. Thus cynicism has now a specific object and becomes a challenge, providing the audience with a basis for action. Associated with it, of course, is utopian optimism with regard to the working class. In extreme form this position has the dryness and coldness of a theorem and it is for this reason that the second phase is the most poetic, since at this point the first and last attitude war with each other in lyrical ambiguity and the poet has not yet committed himself to a closed system.

Brecht composed his ballads to the accompaniment of a guitar. When he worked in the theater (and he is to be credited with reviving serious lyrics in the theater) or the film, he collaborated first with Kurt Weill and later with Hanns Eisler. The songs for the labor movement which were set to music by Eisler are internationally famous. In Germany, in Russia, in France, in Spain during the civil war, even in America they have been sung and marched to by the workers. They have enjoyed a popularity nothing short of amazing in an age in which poetry has tended to become more and more the concern of only a few specialists.

10

In addition to the ballad Brecht has developed an unrhymed type of poetry which he calls *Gestich*. It consists of slightly formalized speech rhythms with certain forced pauses produced by arbitrary line division. In translating it is important to adhere closely to these line divisions in order to preserve a calculated emphasis. The diction of this verse is influenced by the Bible and the compressed simplicity of Chinese poetry. *Gestich* is used by Brecht in many of his plays, and thus the poems in this style can almost be regarded as speeches or choruses from plays. As a functional poet Brecht is inevitably drawn toward the drama. *Gestich* represents a search for a dignified style with a slightly higher tension than prose but simple enough for an audience to follow aurally without difficulty.

When the left movement was destroyed by Nazism it was axiomatic that Brecht should become the spearhead of German literary anti-Nazism. Exiled from the beginning of Hitler's regime, he fled from one Scandinavian country to another, finally escaping from Finland to America just as the former country allied itself with Germany. In exile he continued to let fly his shafts of satire at the Third Reich. This gives much of his poetry a special significance, for it was the expression of German resistance, sometimes broadcast over the Freedom Station, sometimes printed in refugee publications. From his antiwar satires dating from just after the first world war to his bitter dissection of the hypocrisies of fascism, Brecht's voice is the voice of the German conscience. Upon him and writers of similar integrity depends the task of rebuilding German culture.

Brecht's significance as a German and for German cultural reconstruction, however, must not be allowed to overshadow his international importance. The age in which we live is peculiarly marked by economic and political thinking. The catastrophic war from which we have just emerged and the fear of the forces of destruction which are now in our hands allow no one to remain indifferent to the social organization of the world. Brecht has striven to make the role of poetry in our world an active one. He has attempted to forge a dramatic and lyrical expression for some of our gravest problems. In so doing he has created something new.

H. R. HAYS

11

From

HAUSPOSTILLE

VOM ARMEN B. B.

Ich, Bertolt Brecht, bin aus den schwarzen Wäldern.
Meine Mutter trug mich in die Städte hinein
Als ich in ihrem Leibe lag. Und die Kälte der Wälder
Wird in mir bis zu meinem Absterben sein.

In der Asphaltstadt bin ich daheim. Von allem Anfang
Versehen mit jedem Sterbsakrament:
Mit Zeitungen. Und Tabak. Und Branntwein.
Misstrauisch und faul und zufrieden am End.

Ich bin zu den Leuten freundlich. Ich setze
Einen steifen Hut auf nach ihrem Brauch.
Ich sage: es sind ganz besonders riechende Tiere
Und ich sage: es macht nichts, ich bin es auch.

In meine leeren Schaukelstühle vormittags
Setze ich mir mitunter ein paar Frauen
Und ich betrachte sie sorglos und sage ihnen:
In mir habt ihr einen, auf den könnt ihr nicht bauen.

Gegen Abend versammle ich um mich Männer
Wir reden uns da mit „Gentlemen" an
Sie haben ihre Füsse auf meinen Tischen
Und sagen: es wird besser mit uns. Und ich frage nicht: wann.

Gegen Morgen in der grauen Frühe pissen die Tannen
Und ihr Ungeziefer, die Vögel, fängt an zu schrein.
Um die Stunde trink ich mein Glas in der Stadt aus und schmeisse
Den Tabakstummel weg und schlafe beunruhigt ein.

Wir sind gesessen ein leichtes Geschlechte
In Häusern, die für unzerstörbare galten
(So haben wir gebaut die langen Gehäuse des Eilands Manhattan
Und die dünnen Antennen, die das Atlantische Meer unterhalten).

Von diesen Städten wird bleiben: der durch sie hindurchging, der
        Wind!
Fröhlich machet das Haus den Esser: er leert es.
Wir wissen, dass wir Vorläufige sind
Und nach uns wird kommen: nichts Nennenswertes.

14

CONCERNING POOR B. B.

I, Bertolt Brecht, come from the black forests.
My mother carried me to town while in her womb I lay
And still the coldness of the woods lingers
And shall remain in me until my dying day.

I am at home on pavements. From the beginning
Well provided with extreme unction—sacrament
Of newspapers. And tobacco. And likewise brandy.
Mistrustful, lazy, yet in the end content.

I make friends with people. And I wear
A derby on my head as others do.
I say: they're strangely stinking animals.
And I say: no matter, I am, too.

Forenoons in my rocking chair I sit
Between a couple of women, days on end,
And I gaze upon them carelessly and say:
Here you have a man on whom you can't depend.

I gather some fellows around me toward evening:
We address each other as "gentlemen."
They put their feet up on my table
And say: things will improve. And I don't ask when.

Toward morning the fir trees piss in the gray light
And their vermin, the birds, begin to cheep.
At this hour, in town, I empty my glass,
I knock out my pipe and unquietly I sleep.

A fickle race, we have lived in houses
Said to be built indestructibly
(As we reared the tall buildings of Manhattan Island
And the thin antennae that span the Atlantic Sea).

There shall remain of these cities but the wind that blew through
them!
The house maketh the feaster merry: it is emptied out.
We know that we are makeshift
And after us will come—practically nought.

Bei den Erdbeben, die kommen werden, werde ich hoffentlich
Meine Virginia nicht ausgehen lassen durch Bitterkeit,
Ich, Bertolt Brecht, in die Asphaltstädte verschlagen
Aus den schwarzen Wäldern in meiner Mutter in früher Zeit.

In the earthquakes to come it is to be hoped
I shan't allow bitterness to quench my cigar's glow,
I, Bertolt Brecht, astray in cement cities,
Brought from the woods in my mother long ago.

APFELBÖCK ODER DIE LILIE
AUF DEM FELDE

Im milden Lichte Jakob Apfelböck
Erschlug den Vater und die Mutter sein
Und schloss sie beide in den Wäscheschrank
Und blieb im Hause übrig, er allein.

Es schwammen Wolken unterm Himmel hin
Und um sein Haus ging mild der Sommerwind
Und in dem Hause sass er selber drin
Vor sieben Tagen war es noch ein Kind.

Die Tage gingen und die Nacht ging auch
Und nichts war anders ausser mancherlei
Bei seinen Eltern Jakob Apfelböck
Wartete einfach, komme was es sei.

Und als die Leichen rochen aus dem Spind
Da kaufte Jakob eine Azalee
Und Jakob Apfelböck, das arme Kind
Schlief von dem Tag an auf dem Kanapee.

Es bringt die Milchfrau noch die Milch ins Haus
Gerahmte Buttermilch, süss, fett und kühl.
Was er nicht trinkt, das schüttet Jakob aus
Denn Jakob Apfelböck trinkt nicht mehr viel.

Es bringt der Zeitungsmann die Zeitung noch
Mit schwerem Tritt ins Haus beim Abendlicht
Und wirft sie scheppernd in das Kastenloch
Doch Jakob Apfelböck, der liest sie nicht.

Und als die Leichen rochen durch das Haus
Da weinte Jakob und ward krank davon.
Und Jakob Apfelböck zog weinend aus
Und schlief von nun an nur auf dem Balkon.

Es sprach der Zeitungsmann, der täglich kam:
Was riecht hier so? Ich rieche doch Gestank.
In mildem Licht sprach Jakob Apfelböck:
Es ist die Wäsche in dem Wäscheschrank.

APFELBÖCK OR THE LILY OF THE FIELD

In the mild daylight Jacob Apfelböck
Struck his father and his mother down
And shut them both into the laundry chest
And he stayed in the house, he was alone.

Clouds swam up and down beneath the sky,
Around the house a summer wind blew, warm and mild,
And in the house he himself sat
Who seven days ago was still a child.

The days went by and the nights as well,
Though much was changed yet nothing changed at all.
By his parents Jacob Apfelböck simply
Waited for whatever might befall.

And when the bodies reeked within the chest
Then Jacob bought an azalia plant and he,
Jacob Apfelböck, that poor child,
From that day slept on the settee.

The milkwoman still delivered milk,
Skimmed buttermilk, sweet, rich and cool.
What he did not drink he emptied out
For Jacob's appetite was very small.

The newsboy still delivered papers,
With heavy tread at twilight when the day was done
And flung them into the mailbox slot
But Jacob Apfelböck he read not one.

And as the corpses stank through all the house
It made Jacob sick and then he wept
And, weeping, out upon the porch
To sleep, from then on Jacob crept.

Said the newsboy who came each day:
What do I smell? What is this stench?
In the mild daylight Jacob Apfelböck said:
It is the laundry in the laundry chest.

Es sprach die Milchfrau einst, die täglich kam:
Was riecht hier so? Es riecht, als wenn man stirbt!
In mildem Licht sprach Jakob Apfelböck:
Es is das Kalbfleisch, das im Schrank verdirbt.

Und als sie einstens in den Schrank ihm sahn
Stand Jakob Apfelböck in mildem Licht
Und als sie fragten, warum er's getan
Sprach Jakob Apfelböck: Ich weiss es nicht.

Die Milchfrau aber sprach am Tag danach
Ob wohl das Kind einmal, früh oder spät
Ob Jakob Apfelböck wohl einmal noch
Zum Grabe seiner armen Eltern geht?

Said the milkwoman who came each day:
What do I smell? It reeks like something dead.
It is some veal spoiling in the icebox,
In the mild daylight Jacob said.

When, at length, they looked into the chest
And asked him why he struck the blow,
Jacob Apfelböck stood in the mild daylight
And Jacob said: I do not know.

The milkwoman wondered if, sooner or later,
When she spoke of it next day,
Jacob Apfelböck would yet once more
Visit the grave where his poor parents lay.

VON DER KINDESMÖRDERIN, MARIE FARRAR

Marie Farrar, geboren im April
Unmündig, merkmallos, rachitisch, Waise
Bislang angeblich unbescholten, will
Ein Kind ermordet haben in der Weise:
Sie sagt, sie habe schon im zweiten Monat
Bei einer Frau in einem Kellerhaus
Versucht, es abzutreiben mit zwei Spritzen
Angeblich schmerzhaft, doch gings nicht heraus.
Doch ihr, ich bitte euch, wollt nicht in Zorn verfallen
Denn alle Kreatur braucht Hilf von allen.

Sie habe dennoch, sagt sie, gleich bezahlt
Was ausgemacht war, sich fortan geschnürt
Auch Sprit getrunken, Pfeffer drin vermahlt
Doch habe sie das nur stark abgeführt.
Ihr Leib sei zusehends geschwollen, habe
Auch stark geschmerzt, beim Tellerwaschen oft.
Sie selbst sei, sagt sie, damals noch gewachsen.
Sie habe zu Marie gebetet, viel erhofft.
Auch ihr, ich bitte euch, wollt nicht in Zorn verfallen
Denn alle Kreatur braucht Hilf von allen.

Doch die Gebete hätten, scheinbar, nichts genützt.
Es war auch viel verlangt. Als sie dann dicker war
Hab' ihr in Frühmetten geschwindelt. Oft hab' sie geschwitzt.
Auch Angstschweiss, häufig unter dem Altar.
Doch hab' den Zustand sie geheim gehalten
Bis die Geburt sie nachher überfiel.
Es sei gegangen, da wohl niemand glaubte
Dass sie, sehr reizlos, in Versuchung fiel.
Und ihr, ich bitte euch, wollt nicht in Zorn verfallen
Denn alle Kreatur braucht Hilf von allen.

An diesem Tag, sagt sie, in aller Früh
Ist ihr beim Stiegenwaschen so, als krallten
Ihr Nägel in den Bauch. Es schüttelt sie.

CONCERNING THE INFANTICIDE,
MARIE FARRAR

Marie Farrar, born in April,
No marks, a minor, rachitic, both parents dead,
Allegedly, up to now without police record,
Committed infanticide, it is said,
As follows: in her second month, she says,
With the aid of a barmaid she did her best
To get rid of her child with two douches,
Allegedly painful but without success.
But you, I beg you, check your wrath and scorn
For man needs help from every creature born.

She then paid out, she says, what was agreed
And continued to lace herself up tight.
She also drank liquor with pepper mixed in it
Which purged her but did not cure her plight.
Her body distressed her as she washed the dishes,
It was swollen now quite visibly.
She herself says, for she was still a child,
She prayed to Mary most earnestly.
But you, I beg you, check your wrath and scorn
For man needs help from every creature born.

Her prayers, it seemed, helped her not at all.
She longed for help. Her trouble made her falter
And faint at early mass. Often drops of sweat
Broke out in anguish as she knelt at the altar.
Yet until her time had come upon her
She still kept secret her condition.
For no one believed such a thing had happened,
That she, so unenticing, had yielded to temptation.
But you, I beg you, check your wrath and scorn
For man needs help from every creature born.

And on that day, she says, when it was dawn,
As she washed the stairs it seemed a nail
Was driven into her belly. She was wrung with pain.

Jedoch gelingt es ihr, den Schmerz geheim zu halten.
Den ganzen Tag, es ist beim Wäschehängen
Zerbricht sie sich den Kopf; dann kommt sie drauf
Dass sie gebären sollte, und es wird ihr
Gleich schwer ums Herz. Erst spät geht sie hinauf.
Doch ihr, ich bitte euch, wollt nicht in Zorn verfallen
Denn alle Kreatur braucht Hilf von allen.

Man holte sie noch einmal, als sie lag:
Schnee war gefallen und sie musste kehren.
Das ging bis elf. Es war ein langer Tag
Erst in der Nacht konnte sie in Ruhe gebären.
Und sie gebar, so sagt sie, einen Sohn.
Der Sohn war ebenso wie andere Söhne.
Doch sie war nicht so wie die anderen, obschon:
Es liegt kein Grund vor, dass ich sie verhöhne.
Auch ihr, ich bitte euch, wollt nicht in Zorn verfallen
Denn alle Kreatur braucht Hilf von allen.

So will ich also weiter denn erzählen
Wie es mit diesem Sohn geworden ist
(Sie wollte davon, sagt sie, nichts verhehlen).
Damit man sieht, wie ich bin und du bist.
Sie sagt, sie sei, nur kurz im Bett, von Übel-
keit stark befallen worden und, allein
Hab' sie, nicht wissend, was geschehen sollte
Mit Mühe sich bezwungen, nicht zu schrein.
Und ihr, ich bitte euch, wollt nicht in Zorn verfallen
Denn alle Kreatur braucht Hilf von allen.

Mit letzter Kraft hab' sie, so sagt sie, dann
Da ihre Kammer auch eiskalt gewesen
Sich zum Abort geschleppt und dort auch (wann
Weiss sie nicht mehr) geborn ohn Federlesen
So gegen Morgen zu. Sie sei, sagt sie
Jetzt ganz verwirrt gewesen, habe dann
Halb schon erstarrt, das Kind kaum halten können
Weil es in den Gesindabort hereinschnein kann.
Auch ihr, ich bitte euch, wollt nicht in Zorn verfallen
Denn alle Kreatur braucht Hilf von allen.

But still she secretly endured her travail.
All day long while hanging out the laundry
She racked her brains till she got it through her head
She had to bear the child and her heart was heavy.
It was very late when she went up to bed.
But you, I beg you, check your wrath and scorn
For man needs help from every creature born.

She was sent for again as soon as she lay down:
Snow had fallen and she had to go downstairs.
It went on till eleven. It was a long day.
Only at night did she have time to bear.
And so, she says, she gave birth to a son.
The son she bore was just like all the others.
She was unlike the others but for this
There is no reason to despise this mother.
You, too, I beg you, check your wrath and scorn
For man needs help from every creature born.

Accordingly I will go on with the story
Of what happened to the son that came to be.
(She says she will hide nothing that befell)
So let it be a judgment upon both you and me.
She says she had scarcely gone to bed when she
Was overcome with sickness and she was alone,
Not knowing what would happen, yet she still
Contrived to stifle all her moans.
And you, I beg you, check your wrath and scorn
For man needs help from every creature born.

With her last strength, she says, because
Her room had now grown icy cold, she then
Dragged herself to the latrine and there
Gave birth as best she could (not knowing when)
But toward morning. She says she was already
Quite distracted and could barely hold
The child for snow came into the latrine
And her fingers were half numb with cold.
You too, I beg you, check your wrath and scorn
For man needs help from every creature born.

25

Dann zwischen Kammer und Abort, vorher, sagt sie
Sei noch gar nichts gewesen, fing das Kind
Zu schreien an, das hab' sie so verdrossen, sagt sie
Dass sie's mit beiden Fäusten ohne Aufhörn, blind
Solang geschlagen habe, bis es still war, sagt sie.
Hierauf hab' sie das Tote noch gradaus
Zu sich ins Bett genommen für den Rest der Nacht
Und es versteckt am Morgen in dem Wäschehaus.
Doch ihr, ich bitte euch, wollt nicht in Zorn verfallen
Denn alle Kreatur braucht Hilf von allen.

Marie Farrar, geboren im April
Gestorben im Gefängnishaus zu Meissen
Ledige Kindesmutter, abgeurteilt, will
Euch die Gebrechen aller Kreatur erweisen.
Ihr, die ihr gut gebärt in saubern Wochenbetten
Und nennt „gesegnet" euren schwangeren Schoss
Wollt nicht verdammen die verworfnen Schwachen
Denn ihre Sünd war schwer, doch ihr Leid gross.
Darum, ich bitte euch, wollt nicht in Zorn verfallen
Denn alle Kreatur braucht Hilf von allen.

Between the latrine and her room, she says,
Not earlier, the child began to cry until
It drove her mad so that she says
She did not cease to beat it with her fists
Blindly for some time till it was still.
And then she took the body to her bed
And kept it with her there all through the night:
When morning came she hid it in the shed.
But you, I beg you, check your wrath and scorn
For man needs help from every creature born.

Marie Farrar, born in April,
An unmarried mother, convicted, died in
The Meissen penitentiary,
She brings home to you all men's sin.
You who bear pleasantly between clean sheets
And give the name "blessed" to your womb's weight
Must not damn the weakness of the outcast,
For her sin was black but her pain was great.
Therefore, I beg you, check your wrath and scorn
For man needs help from every creature born.

BERICHT VOM ZECK

Durch unsere Kinderträume
In dem milchweissen Bett
Spukte um Apfelbäume
Der Mann in Violett.

Liegend vor ihm im Staube
Sah man: da sass er. Träg.
Und streichelte seine Taube
Und sonnte sich am Weg.

Er schätzt die kleinste Gabe
Sauft Blut als wie ein Zeck.
Und dass man nur ihn habe
Nimmt er sonst alles weg.

Und gabst du für ihn deine
Und Anderer Freude her;
Und liegst dann arm am Steine
Dann kennt er dich nicht mehr.

Er spuckt dir gern zum Spasse
Ins Antlitz rein und guckt
Dass er dich ja gleich fasse
Wenn deine Wimper zuckt.

Am Abend steht er spähend
An deinem Fenster dort
Und merkt sich jedes Lächeln
Und geht beleidigt fort.

Und hast du eine Freude
Und lachst du noch so leis—
Er hat eine kleine Orgel
Drauf spielt er Trauerweis'.

Er taucht in Himmelsbläue
Wenn einer ihn verlacht
And hat doch auch die Haie
Nach seinem Bild gemacht.

ACCOUNT OF THE TICK

All through our childhood fancies,
In our milk-white bed,
A phantom haunts the apple trees,
The man in violet.

Prone in the dust before him
We see him sit. At ease.
Stroking his doves' feathers
And sunning in the trees.

The smallest gifts he prizes,
He sucks blood like a tick.
That you may have him only
He strips you of all else.

And if you barter for him
Your own and others' joy
And on the stones lie needy
He quickly says good-by.

For a joke his spits directly
In your face and peeks
To catch you at the moment
When your eyelash flicks.

At evening he stands spying
Through the windowpane
And when he sees you smiling
In pique he leaves again.

And if some joy is yours,
Though you laugh very low,
He has a little organ
And plays a song of woe.

In blue sky he vanishes
If you laugh him to scorn
And the shark is molded
In his very form.

An keinem sitzt er lieber
Als einst am Totenbett.
Er spukt durchs letzte Fieber
Der Kerl in Violett.

Of death beds he is fondest,
At these he likes to sit.
He haunts a man's last fever,
The chap in violet.

BALLADE VON DES CORTEZ LEUTEN

Am siebten Tage unter leichten Winden
Wurden die Wiesen heller. Da die Sonne gut war
Gedachten sie zu rasten. Rollen Branntwein
Von den Gefährten, koppeln Ochsen los.
Die schlachten sie gen Abend. Als es kühl wird
Schlägt man vom Holz des nachbarlichen Sumpfes
Armdicke Äste, knorrig, gut zu brennen.
Dann schlingen sie gewürztes Fleisch hinunter
Und fangen singend um die neunte Stunde
Mit Trinken an. Die Nacht ist kühl und grün.
Mit heiserer Kehle, tüchtig vollgesogen
Mit einem letzten, kühlen Blick nach grossen Sternen
Entschlafen sie gen Mitternacht am Feuer.
Sie schlafen schwer, doch mancher wusste morgens
Dass er die Ochsen einmal brüllen hörte.
Erwacht gen Mittag, sind sie schon im Wald.
Mit glasigen Augen, schweren Gliedern, heben
Sie ächzend sich aufs Knie und sehen staunend
Armdicke Äste, knorrig, um sie stehen
Höher als mannshoch, sehr verwirrt, mit Blattwerk
Und kleinen Blüten süsslichen Geruchs.
Es ist sehr schwül schon unter ihrem Dach
Das sich zu dichten scheint. Die heisse Sonne
Ist nicht zu sehen, auch der Himmel nicht.
Der Hauptman brüllt laut wie ein Stier nach Äxten
Die lagen drüben, wo die Ochsen brüllten.
Man sah sie nicht. Mit rauhem Fluchen stolpern
Die Leute im Geviert, ans Astwerk stossend
Das zwischen ihnen durchgekrochen war.
Mit schlaffen Armen werfen sie sich wild
In die Gewächse, die leicht zitterten
Als ginge leichter Wind von aussen durch sie.
Nach Stunden Arbeit pressen sie die Stirnen
Schweissglänzend finster an die fremden Äste.
Die Äste wuchsen und vermehrten langsam

32

BALLAD OF CORTEZ' MEN

Upon the seventh day light winds came up;
The meadows then grew bright. Since the sun was strong
They thought to rest. They roll their brandykegs
Out of the carts, the oxen are uncoupled.
They slaughter them toward evening. As it grows chilly,
Within the forest of a neighboring swamp
They cut boughs, thick as a man's arm, knotty
And good for burning. They put away spiced meat
And, singing, at the ninth hour, set about
Their drinking. The night was cool and green.
Their throats yelled hoarse, now thoroughly sodden,
And with a last cold look toward the great stars,
They go to sleep toward midnight at the fire.
They sleep heavily, yet many in the morning
Knew they had heard the oxen bellowing.
Waking at midday they are still in the forest.
With glassy eyes and heavy limbs they get
Groaning to their feet and see, amazedly,
Boughs, thick as a man's arm and knotty, standing
Higher than their heads, much intertwined with foliage
And little blossoms having a sweet smell.
Already it is very sultry under their new roof
Which seems too thick to them. Even the hot sun
Is invisible. They cannot see the sky.
The captain bellows like a steer for axes.
They lie yonder where the oxen bellowed,
Not to be seen. The soldiers with rough curses
Stagger in the maze, pushing against the boughs
That have crept in all amongst them. At once
With thrashing arms they wildly fling themselves
Into the bushes which are trembling gently
As if a light wind blew through them from outside.
After hours of labor they thrust their foreheads,
Darkly bright with sweat, against the strange limbs.
The boughs grow taller and the fearful tangle

Das schreckliche Gewirr. Später, am Abend
Der dunkler war, weil oben Blattwerk wuchs
Sitzen sie schweigend, angstvoll und wie Affen
In ihren Käfigen, von Hunger matt.
Nachts wuchs das Astwerk. Doch es musste Mond sein
Es war noch ziemlich hell, sie sahn sich noch.
Erst gegen Morgen war das Zeug so dick
Dass sie sich nimmer sahen, bis sie starben.
Den Nächsten Tag stieg Singen aus dem Wald.
Dumpf und verhallt. Sie sangen sich wohl zu.
Nachts ward es stiller. Auch die Ochsen schwiegen.
Gen Morgen war es, als ob Tiere brüllten
Doch ziemlich weit weg. Später kamen Stunden
Wo es ganz still war. Langsam frass der Wald
In leichtem Wind, bei guter Sonne, still
Die Wiesen in den nächsten Wochen auf.

Slowly increases. Later in the evening,
Which is darker, while over them the foliage grows,
They sit silent, full of anguish, like apes
Shut up in cages, weak from hunger. At night
The boughs kept growing. Since it was moonlight,
There was still some brightness. They could see each other.
At last, toward morning, the stuff had grown so thick
They saw each other no more till they died.
The next day singing rose up out of the woods,
Muffled and hollow. They must have sung to themselves.
At night it grew quieter. The oxen, too, were silent.
Toward morning it was as if beasts bellowed
Yet rather far away. A time came later
When all was still. Slowly the forest,
Under the strong sun while a light wind blew,
Silently, in the next weeks, ate the meadows up.

DIE BALLADE VON DEM SOLDATEN

Das Schiessgewehr schiesst und das Spiessmesser spiesst
Und das Wasser frisst auf, die drin waten.
Was könnt ihr gegen Eis? Bleibt weg, 's ist nicht weis'!
Sagte das Weib zum Soldaten.

Doch der Soldat mit der Kugel im Lauf
Hörte die Trommel und lachte darauf
Marschieren kann nimmermehr schaden!
Hinab nach dem Süden, nach dem Norden hinauf
Und das Messer fängt er mit Händen auf!
Sagten zum Weib die Soldaten.

Ach, bitter bereut, wer des Weisen Rat scheut
Und vom Alter sich nicht lässt beraten!
Ach, zu hoch nicht hinaus, es geht übel aus!
Sagte das Weib zum Soldaten.

Doch der Soldat mit dem Messer im Gurt
Lacht ihr kalt ins Gesicht und ging über die Furt
Was konnte das Wasser ihm schaden?
Wenn weiss der Mond überm Mongefluss steht
Kommen wir wieder; nimm's auf ins Gebet!
Sagten zum Weib die Soldaten.

Ihr vergeht wie der Rauch, und die Wärme geht auch
Und uns wärmen nicht eure Taten!
Ach, wie schnell geht der Rauch! Gott, behüte ihn auch!
Sagte das Weib vom Soldaten.

Und der Soldat mit dem Messer am Gurt
Sank hin mit dem Speer, und mit riss ihn die Furt
Und das Wasser frass auf, die drin waten.
Kühl stand der Mond überm Mongefluss weiss
Doch der Soldat trieb hinab mit dem Eis
Und was sagten dem Weib die Soldaten?

Er verging wie der Rauch, und die Wärme ging auch
Und es wärmten sie nicht seine Taten.
Ach bitter bereut, wer des Weibes Rat scheut!
Sagte das Weib zum Soldaten.

BALLAD OF THE SOLDIER

The trigger will shoot and the dagger will strike,
If you wade in the water 'twill freeze you.
Watch out for the ice, keep out if you're wise,
Said the goodwife to the soldier.

But the soldier boy with his weapons in place
Harked to the drumming and laughed in her face.
For bugles and drums never hurt you.
From the north to the south he'll march all his life
And his fingers were made just to handle a knife,
The soldiers they said to the goodwife.

Oh bitter you'll mourn the counsel you scorn
When you turn a deaf ear to your elders.
In God's name here abide, there's danger outside,
Said the goodwife to the soldier.

But the soldier boy, with his pistol and sword,
Laughed aloud at her words and crossed over the ford,
For how could the cold water hurt him?
When the moon glimmers white on the crest of the knoll,
You shall see us again. Now pray for his soul,
The soldiers they said to the goodwife.

You are gone like smoke. And the heat is gone, too.
For your glory can never warm us.
How quick the smoke goes! Then God preserve you,
Said the goodwife of the soldier.

And the soldier boy with his pistol and sword
Sank down with the spear and was lost in the ford
And he waded in water that froze him.
And cool on the crest the moon shone white
But the soldier and ice whirled away in the night
And then what did they say to the goodwife?

He is gone like smoke and the heat is gone, too
And his deeds will never warm her.
Oh bitter to mourn women's counsel you scorn,
Said the goodwife to the soldier.

DAS LIED VON DER EISENBAHN-
TRUPPE VON FORT DONALD

Die Männer von Fort Donald—hohé!
Zogen den Strom hinauf, bis die Wälder ewig und seelenlos sind.
Aber eines Tags ging Regen nieder und der Wald wuchs um sie zum
    See.
Sie standen im Wasser bis an die Knie.
Und der Morgen kommt nie, sagten sie
Und wir versaufen vor der Früh, sagten sie
Und sie horchten stumm auf den Eriewind.

Die Männer von Fort Donald—hohé!
Standen am Wasser mit Pickel und Schiene und schauten zum dunk-
    leren Himmel hinauf
Denn es ward dunkel und der Abend wuchs aus dem plätschernden See.
Ach, kein Fetzen Himmel, der Hoffnung lieh
Und wir sind schon müd, sagten sie
Und wir schlafen noch ein, sagten sie
Und uns weckt keine Sonne mehr auf.

Die Männer von Fort Donald—hohé!
Sagten gleich: wenn wir einschlafen, sind wir adje!
Denn Schlaf wuchs aus Wasser und Nacht, und sie waren voll Furcht
    wie Vieh
Einer sagte: singt „Johnny über der See."
Ja, das hält uns vielleicht auf, sagten sie
Ja, wir singen seinen Song, sagten sie
Und sie sangen von Johnny über der See.

Die Männer von Fort Donald—hohé!
Tappten in diesem dunklen Ohio wie Maulwürfe blind
Aber sie sangen so laut, als ob ihnen wunder was Angenehmes
    geschäh
Ja, so sangen sie nie.
Oh, wo ist mein Johnny zur Nacht, sangen sie
Oh, wo ist mein Johnny zur Nacht, sangen sie
Und das nasse Ohio wuchs unten, und oben wuchs Regen und Wind.

SONG OF THE RAILROAD GANG
OF FORT DONALD

The men of Fort Donald—yessiree!
Traveled upstream to where the woods are pitiless and blind.
But one day the rain came down and about them the woods turned
    into a sea
And they stood in water up to the knee.
And tomorrow will never come, said they.
And we shall drown before dawn, said they.
And they hearkened dumbly to the Erie wind.

The men of Fort Donald—yessiree!
Stood in the water with rails and picks and looked into the black sky.
For it was dark and evening arose out of the splashing sea
And no hopeful break in the cloudy heavens could they see.
And we are tired, said they.
And we shall fall asleep, said they.
And we shall not awaken when the sun is high.

The men of Fort Donald—yessiree!
Likewise said: we are done for if we fall asleep!
For sleep rose out of the water and the night and they were panic-
    stricken as sheep
Till one said: sing "Johnny Over the Sea."
Yes, we might be able to hold out, said they.
Yes, we will sing your song, said they.
And they sang of Johnny over the sea.

The men of Fort Donald—yessiree!
Groped like moles in the darkness, lost and blind,
But they sang as loud as if some joyous marvel had come to be,
Never had they sung this way.
Oh, where is my Johnny tonight, sang they.
Oh, where is my Johnny tonight, sang they.
And around them the wet Ohio rose and above them the rain and
    the wind.

Die Männer von Fort Donald—hohé!
Werden jetzt wachen und singen, bis sie ersoffen sind.
Doch das Wasser ist höher als sie bis zur Früh und lauter als sie der
  Eriewind schrie
Wo is mein Johnny zur Nacht, sangen sie
Dieser Ohio ist nass, sagten sie
Früh wachte nur noch das Wasser und nur noch der Eriewind.

Die Männer von Fort Donald—hohé!
Die Züge sausen über sie weg an den Eriesee
Und der Wind an der Stelle singt eine dumme Melodie
Und die Kiefern schrein den Zügen nach: hohé!
Damals kam der Morgen nie, schreien sie
Ja, sie versoffen vor der Früh, schreien sie
Unser Wind singt abends oft noch ihren Johnny über der See.

The men of Fort Donald—yessiree!
Now they shall wake and sing until they are washed away.
For the water is higher than they at dawn and the wind shrieks
    louder than they.
Where is my Johnny tonight, sang they.
The Ohio River is wet, said they.
At dawn only the water was wakeful, only water and the Erie wind.

The men of Fort Donald—yessiree!
The trains whistle over them along Lake Erie
And the wind over the spot sings a stupid melody
And the pine trees shriek after the train: yessiree!
For morning never came, they cry.
Yes, they were drowned before dawn, they cry.
At evening our wind often sings of their Johnny over the sea.

BALLADE VON DEN ABENTEURERN

Von Sonne krank und ganz von Regen zerfressen
Geraubten Lorbeer im zerrauften Haar
Hat er seine ganze Jugend, nur nicht ihre Träume vergessen
Lange das Dach, nie den Himmel, der drüber war.

O ihr, die ihr aus Himmel und Hölle vertrieben
Ihr Mörder, denen viel Leides geschah
Warum seid ihr nicht im Schoss eurer Mütter geblieben
Wo es stille war und man schlief und man war da?

Er aber sucht noch in absinthenen Meeren
Wenn ihn schon seine Mutter vergisst
Grinsend und fluchend und zuweilen nicht ohne Zähren
Immer das Land, wo es besser zu leben ist.

Schlendernd durch Höllen und gepeitscht durch Paradiese
Still und grinsend vergehenden Gesichts
Träumt er gelegentlich von einer kleinen Wiese
Mit blauem Himmel drüber und sonst nichts.

BALLAD OF THE ADVENTURERS

Sick from sun, by rainy weather battered,
With stolen laurels, his fierce hair torn,
His youth, not its dreams, he has forgotten,
The roof, not the sky, under which he was born.

O you, who are driven from hell and from heaven,
O murderers sorely afflicted with grief,
Why did you not linger in the womb of your mother
Where it was silent and you slept in peace?

But still he is seeking in seas of absinthe,
When even his mother forgets his face,
Amid sneers and curses and sometimes with sobs,
Forever seeking a happier place.

Strolling through hell, scourged through Paradise,
Silent and grimacing the face goes by.
Now and then he dreams of a little meadow
And nothing else except blue sky.

ERINNERUNG AN DIE MARIE A.

An jenem Tag im blauen Mond September
Still unter einem jungen Pflaumenbaum
Da hielt ich sie, die stille bleiche Liebe
In meinem Arm wie einen holden Traum.
Und über uns im schönen Sommerhimmel
War eine Wolke, die ich flüchtig sah
Sie war sehr weiss und ungeheuer oben
Und als ich aufsah, war sie nimmer da.

Seit jenem Tag sind viele, viele Monde
Geschwommen still hinunter und vorbei
Die Pflaumenbäume sind wohl abgehauen
Und fragst du mich, was mit der Liebe sei?
So sag ich dir: ich kann mich nicht erinnern.
Und doch, gewiss, ich weiss schon, was du meinst
Doch ihr Gesicht, das weiss ich wirklich nimmer
Ich weiss nur mehr: Ich küsste es dereinst.

Und auch den Kuss, ich hätt' ihn längst vergessen
Wenn nicht die Wolke da gewesen wär
Die weiss ich noch und werd ich immer wissen
Sie war sehr weiss und kam von oben her.
Die Pflaumenbäume blühn vielleicht noch immer
Und jene Frau hat jetzt vielleicht das siebte Kind
Doch jene Wolke blühte nur Minuten
Und als ich aufsah, schwand sie schon im Wind.

IN MEMORY OF MARIE A.

One day in the blue month of September
Silently I held her under a young plum tree,
I held her there, my pale and silent loved one,
And like a gentle dream within my arms was she.
And over us in the fair summer heavens
Was a cloud that fleetingly I saw,
Very white and terribly far above us,
And as I looked up it was there no more.

Since that day so many, many months
Have silently swum by and are no more.
No doubt the plum trees have been all cut down.
And if you ask me what became of her
I'll tell you truly that I don't remember.
I know already why you ask me this,
And yet her face I really have forgotten,
I know no more of it than that one kiss.

Even the kiss I should have quite forgotten
If there had been no cloud there, long ago.
I see it still and I shall always see it
For it was white and drifted down like snow.
Perhaps the plum trees bear their yearly blossoms,
Perhaps the woman has her seventh child,
And yet that cloud bloomed only for a minute
And as I looked up vanished in the wind.

VOM SCHWIMMEN IN SEEN
UND FLÜSSEN

Im bleichen Sommer, wenn die Winde oben
Nur in dem Laub der grossen Bäume sausen
Muss man in Flüssen liegen oder Teichen
Wie die Gewächse, worin Hechte hausen.
Der Leib wird leicht im Wasser. Wenn der Arm
Leicht aus dem Wasser in den Himmel fällt
Wiegt ihn der kleine Wind vergessen
Weil er ihn wohl für braunes Astwerk hält.

Der Himmel bietet mittags grosse Stille.
Man macht die Augen zu, wenn Schwalben kommen.
Der Schlamm ist warm. Wenn kühle Blasen quellen
Weiss man: ein Fisch ist jetzt durch uns geschwommen.
Mein Leib, die Schenkel und der stille Arm
Wir liegen still im Wasser, ganz geeint
Nur wenn die kühlen Fische durch uns schwimmen
Fühl ich, dass Sonne überm Tümpel scheint.

Wenn man am Abend von dem langen Liegen
Sehr faul wird, so, dass alle Glieder beissen
Muss man das alles, ohne Rücksicht, klatschend
In blaue Flüsse schmeissen, die sehr reissen.
Am besten ist's, man hält's bis Abend aus.
Weil dann der bleiche Haifischhimmel kommt
Bös und gefrässig über Fluss und Sträuchern
Und alle Dinge sind, wie's ihnen frommt.

Natürlich muss man auf dem Rücken liegen
So wie gewöhnlich. Und sich treiben lassen.
Man muss nicht schwimmen, nein, nur so tun, als
Gehöre man einfach zu Schottermassen.
Man soll den Himmel anschaun und so tun
Als ob einen ein Weib trägt, und es stimmt.
Ganz ohne grossen Umtrieb, wie der liebe Gott tut
Wenn er am Abend noch in seinen Flüssen schwimmt.

OF SWIMMING IN LAKES
AND RIVERS

In the pale summertime, when far above you
In only the largest trees the winds are sighing,
You must float inert in a pool or in a river
Like the waterweeds in which pike are lying.
Your flesh grows light in water. Thrust your arm
Softly from water into air and now
The little wind cradles it forgetfully,
Seeming to take it for a brown bough.

At midday the sky proffers a great stillness.
You close your eyes when the swallows pass you.
The mud is warm. When the cool bubbles rise up
You know that a fish has just swum across you.
Your body, your thigh and motionless arm
Lie in quiet unity, only when the cool
Fish are swimming lazily across you
Can you feel the sun shine down upon the pool.

In the evening when, from long lying,
You grow so lazy that all your limbs prickle
Without a backward glance you must fling yourself,
Splashing, into a blue river where the rapids ripple.
It is best to hold out until evening comes
For then, like a shark over stream and shrubbery,
The pale sky looms, angry and gluttonous,
And all things are just as they should be.

You must, of course, lie on your back quietly
As is usual and let yourself go on drifting.
You must not swim, no, but only act as if
You were a mass of flotsam slowly shifting.
You must look up at the sky and act as if
A woman carried you, and it is so.
Quiet, without disturbance, as the good God himself **does**
When at evening he swims in his rivers here below.

VOM ERTRUNKENEN MÄDCHEN

Als sie ertrunken war und hinunterschwamm
Von den Bächen in die grösseren Flüsse
Schien der Opal des Himmels sehr wundersam
Als ob er die Leiche begütigen müsse.

Tang und Algen hielten sich an ihr ein
So dass sie langsam viel schwerer ward
Kühl die Fische schwammen an ihrem Bein
Pflanzen und Tiere beschwerten noch ihre letzte Fahrt.

Und der Himmel ward abends dunkel wie Rauch
Und hielt nachts mit den Sternen das Licht in Schwebe.
Aber früh war er hell, dass es auch
Noch für sie Morgen und Abend gebe.

Als ihr bleicher Leib im Wasser verfaulet war,
Geschah es (sehr langsam), dass Gott sie allmählich vergass
Erst ihr Gesicht, dann die Hände und ganz zuletzt erst ihr Haar.
Dann ward sie Aas in Flüssen mit vielem Aas.

CONCERNING A DROWNED GIRL

As she was drowned and drifted down
From brooks to where the streams grew broader,
The opal of the sky shone strangely fair
As if some comfort to accord her.

Weeds and algae clung about the corpse
Until they slowly weighted down the maiden.
Cool fish swam about her legs till she,
On her last trip, with plant and beast was laden.

Evenings the sky grew dark as smoke,
At night the stars held light suspended.
And early it grew bright and still for her
Morning and evening were not ended.

As her pale body rotted in the river,
It happened (very slowly) that God forgot her,
First her face, her hands, at last her hair.
Then she was carrion with the carrion in the water.

LIED AM SCHWARZEN SAMSTAG IN DER ELFTEN STUNDE DER NACHT VOR OSTERN

Im Frühjahr unter grünen Himmeln, wilden
Verliebten Winden schon etwas vertiert
Fuhr ich hinunter in die schwarzen Städte
Mit kalten Sprüchen innen tapeziert.

Ich füllte mich mit schwarzen Asphalttieren
Ich füllte mich mit Wasser und Geschrei
Mich aber liess es kalt und leicht, mein Lieber
Ich blieb ganz ungefüllt und leicht dabei.

Sie schlugen Löcher wohl in meine Wände
Und krochen fluchend wieder aus von mir:
Es war nichts drinnen als viel Platz and Stille
Sie schrieen fluchend: ich sei nur Papier.

Ich rollte feixend abwärts zwischen Häusern
Hinaus ins Freie. Leis und feierlich
Lief jetzt der Wind schneller durch meine Wände
Es schneite noch. Es regnete in mich.

Zynischer Burschen arme Rüssel haben
Gefunden, dass in mir nichts ist.
Wildsäue haben sich in mir begattet. Raben
Des milchigen Himmels oft in mich gepisst.

Schwächer als Wolken! Leichter als die Winde!
Nicht sichtbar! Leicht, vertiert und feierlich
Wie ein Gedicht von mir, flog ich durch Himmel
Mit einem Storch, der etwas schneller strich!

SONG ON BLACK SATURDAY AT THE ELEVENTH HOUR OF THE NIGHT BEFORE EASTER

In the springtime, under a green sky, already
Somewhat brutal, wild loved winds I buried
Within me as I entered the blackness of the cities,
Upholstery of cold proverbs in me I carried.

I filled myself with beasts from the black pavements,
I filled myself with water and with loud outcry,
But it left me very cold and light, my boy,
Utterly unfulfilled and light was I.

Indeed they knocked holes through all my walls
And, cursing, crept outside of me again:
There was nothing in me but much space and silence,
I was nought but paper: they shrieked, and cursed me then.

Grinning, I rolled down between the houses
Into the open, soft and festively
The wind blew—more swiftly through my walls,
And still it snowed. It rained in me.

The mean snouts of cynical fellows have discovered
That in me nothing at all exists.
Wild swine have paired in me. Often in me
Out of milky heavens ravens have pissed.

Frailer than clouds! Lighter than the winds!
Invisible! Light, brutal and gay the while,
Like one of my poems, I flew through the heavens
With a stork that flapped in somewhat quicker style!

LITURGIE VOM HAUCH

Einst kam ein altes Weib einher
Die hatte kein Brot zum Essen mehr
Das Brot, das frass das Militär
Da fiel sie in die Goss', die war kalte.
Da hatte sie keinen Hunger mehr.

      Darauf schwiegen die Vöglein im Walde
      Über allen Wipfeln ist Ruh
      In allen Gipfeln spürest du
      Kaum einen Hauch.

Da kam einmal ein Totenarzt einher
Der sagte: die Alte besteht auf ihrem Schein
Da grub man die hungrige Alte ein
So sagte das alte Weib nichts mehr.
Nur der Arzt lachte noch über die Alte.

      Auch die Vöglein schwiegen im Walde
      Über allen Wipfeln ist Ruh
      In allen Gipfeln spürest du
      Kaum einen Hauch.

Da kam einmal ein einziger Mann einher
Der hatte für die Ordnung gar keinen Sinn
Der fand in der Sache einen Haken drin
Der war eine Art Freund für die Alte.
Der sagte, ein Mensch müsse essen können, bitte sehr—

      Darauf schwiegen die Vöglein im Walde
      Über allen Wipfeln ist Ruh
      In allen Gipfeln spürest du
      Kaum einen Hauch.

Da kam mit einemmal ein Kommissar einher
Der hatte einen Gummiknüppel dabei
Und zerklopfte dem Mann seinen Hinterkopf zu Brei
Und da sagte auch dieser Mann nichts mehr.
Doch der Kommissar sagte, dass es schallte:

LITANY OF BREATH

There came an old wife down the street:
She hadn't a piece of bread to eat
Because the soldiers gobbled the wheat.
She fell in the cold, cold gutter
And then she wanted no more to eat.

> *About this the little birds were silent in the forest.*
> *Over all the mountains is rest:*
> *In all the treetops you perceive*
> *Scarcely a breath.*

There came a doctor down the street
Who called the old woman an obstinate fraud.
They buried her then, she was stiff as a board.
All the while she said not a word.
But the doctor he laughed about the old woman.

> *Also the little birds were silent in the forest.*
> *Over all the mountains is rest:*
> *In all the treetops you perceive*
> *Scarcely a breath.*

There came one man down the street.
He saw no sense in what happened there,
He found the catch in the whole affair.
He was the old woman's friend in a way.
He said, if you please, people really must eat.

> *About this the little birds were silent in the forest.*
> *Over all the mountains is rest:*
> *In all the treetops you perceive*
> *Scarcely a breath.*

There came an inspector down the street.
He had a rubber club loaded with lead:
He smashed in the back of that man's head
And not another word he said.
But the inspector said so it echoed:

53

So! jetzt schweigen die Vögelein im Walde
Über allen Wipfeln ist Ruh
In allen Gipfeln spürest du
Kaum einen Hauch.

Da kamen einmal drei bärtige Männer einher.
Die sagten, das sei nicht eines einzigen Mannes Sache allein.
Und sie sagten es so lang bis es knallte
Aber dann krochen Maden durch ihr Fleisch in ihr Bein.
Da sagten die bärtigen Männer nichts mehr.

Darauf schwiegen die Vögelein im Walde
Über allen Wipfeln ist Ruh
In allen Gipfeln spürest du
Kaum einen Hauch.

Da kamen mit einemmal viele rote Männer einher
Die wollten einmal reden mit dem Militär
Doch das Militär redete mit dem Maschinengewehr
Und da sagten die roten Männer nichts mehr.
Doch sie hatten auf ihrer Stirn noch eine Falte.

Darauf schwiegen die Vögelein im Walde
Über allen Wipfeln ist Ruh
In allen Gipfeln spürest du
Kaum einen Hauch.

Da kam einmal ein grosser roter Bär einher
Der wusste nichts von den Bräuchen hier, denn der kam von überm
Meer
Und der frass die Vögelein im Walde.

Da schwiegen die Vöglein nicht mehr
Über allen Wipfeln ist Unruh
In allen Gipfeln spürest du
Jetzt einen Hauch.

There! Now the little birds are silent in the forest.
Over all the mountains is rest:
In all the treetops you perceive
Scarcely a breath.

There came three bearded men down the street.
They said this can't be cured by one man alone.
And they said it till it echoed louder than before.
But then maggots crept through their flesh to the bone
And the bearded men said nothing more.

About this the little birds were silent in the forest.
Over all the mountains is rest:
In all the treetops you perceive
Scarcely a breath.

Then many workers came down the street.
They wanted to talk to the soldiers, they said.
But the soldiers talked with machine-gun lead
And the workers they could no longer speak
But they died with wrinkled foreheads.

About this the little birds were silent in the forest.
Over all the mountains is rest:
In all the treetops you perceive
Scarcely a breath.

A fine big bear came down the street.
He knew nothing of these customs: he came from a land of snow
    and sleet.
And he gobbled up the little birds in the forest.

About this the little birds were silent no longer.
Over every mountain is unrest:
In all the treetops you perceive
Distinctly a breath.

LEGENDE VOM TOTEN SOLDATEN

Und als der Krieg im fünften Lenz
Keinen Ausblick auf Frieden bot
Da zog der Soldat seine Konsequenz
Und starb den Heldentod.

Der Krieg war aber noch nicht gar
Drum tat es dem Kaiser leid
Dass sein Soldat gestorben war:
Es schien ihm noch vor der Zeit.

Der Sommer zog über die Gräber her
Und der Soldat schlief schon
Da kam eines Nachts eine militär-
ische ärztliche Kommission.

Es zog die ärztliche Kommission
Zum Gottesacker hinaus
Und grub mit geweihtem Spaten den
Gefallnen Soldaten aus.

Und der Doktor besah den Soldaten genau
Oder was von ihm noch da war
Und der Doktor fand, der Soldat war k. v.
Und er drücke sich vor der Gefahr.

Und sie nahmen sogleich den Soldaten mit
Die Nacht war blau und schön.
Man konnte, wenn man keinen Helm aufhatte
Die Sterne der Heimat sehn.

Sie schütteten ihm einen feurigen Schnaps
In den verwesten Leib
Und hängten zwei Schwestern in seinen Arm
Und sein halb entblösstes Weib.

Und weil der Soldat nach Verwesung stinkt
Drum hinkt ein Pfaffe voran
Der über ihn ein Weihrauchfass schwingt
Dass er nicht stinken kann.

LEGEND OF THE DEAD SOLDIER

And when the fifth springtime of war
No sign of peace brought forth
The soldier said: you can go to hell,
And died a hero's death.

Because the war was not quite done
It made the Kaiser blue
To think the soldier lay there dead
Before his time came due.

Summer flowed across the graves
And the soldier he slept on.
And then one day there came a mil-
itary medical commissión.

The medical commission trailed out
To the little acre of God
And with sanctified spades they dug the fallen
Soldier out of the sod.

The doctor looked him over well
Or what was left to see.
The doctor found he was O.K.,
A shirking coward he.

They took the soldier along with them,
The night was blue and fine.
You could—without a helmet on—
Have seen the stars of home.

With fiery schnapps they tried to rouse
His rotted limbs to life.
They hung two nurses on his arms
And his half-naked wife.

And since the soldier stank of rot
A priest limped on before
Who waved an incense burner about
So he should stink no more.

Voran die Musik mit Tschindrara
Spielt einen flotten Marsch.
Und der Soldat, so wie er's gelernt
Schmeisst seine Beine vom Arsch.

Und brüderlich den Arm um ihm
Zwei Sanitäter gehn
Sonst flög er noch in den Dreck ihnen hin
Und das darf nicht geschehn.

Sie malten auf sein Leichenhemd
Die Farben schwarz-weiss-rot
Und trugen's vor ihm her; man sah
Vor Farben nicht mehr den Kot.

Ein Herr in Frack schritt auch voran
Mit einer gestärkten Brust
Der war sich als ein deutscher Mann
Seiner Pflicht genau bewusst.

So zogen sie mit Tschindrara
Hinab die dunkle Chaussee
Und der Soldat zog taumelnd mit
Wie im Sturm die Flocke Schnee.

Die Katzen und die Hunde schrein
Die Ratzen im Feld pfeifen wüst:
Sie wollen nicht französisch sein
Weil das eine Schande ist.

Und wenn sie durch die Dörfer ziehn
Waren alle Weiber da.
Die Bäume verneigten sich. Vollmond schien.
Und alles schrie hurra!

Mit Tschindrara und Wiedersehn!
Und Weib und Hund und Pfaff!
Und mitten drin der tote Soldat
Wie ein besoffner Aff.

In front the music with tzing-boom-boom
Played a jolly march
And the soldier, the way he was taught,
Swung his legs from the arse.

Arms linked in his, two whitewings walked
And held him tenderly
For he would have slipped down in the mud
And that must never be.

They painted colors on his shroud,
Red, white and black,
And carried the colors on before
So no one saw the muck.

A man in tails strode on ahead,
His chest was bulging, too,
For as a German citizen
He knew just what to do.

And marching then with tzing-boom-boom
Down the dark high road they go
And the soldier reeled as in a storm
Like a pale flake of snow.

The cats and dogs began to howl,
The field rats squeaked at him.
They wouldn't think of being French
Because it was a sin.

And when they passed through villages
The women all were there.
The trees bowed low. The full moon shone.
And all cried out: hurrah!

With tzing-boom-boom and fare-thee-well,
With priest and dog and dame—
And in the middle like a drunken ape
The fallen soldier came.

Und wenn sie durch die Dörfer ziehn
Kommt's, dass ihn keiner sah
So viele waren herum um ihn
Mit Tschindra und Hurra.

So viele tanzten und johlten um ihn
Dass ihn keiner sah.
Man konnte ihn einzig von oben noch sehr
Und da sind nur Sterne da.

Die Sterne sind nicht immer da.
Es kommt ein Morgenrot.
Doch der Soldat, so wie er's gelernt
Zieht in den Heldentod.

And when they passed through villages
The crowd it left no room
To see the soldier, so many ran
With hurrah and tzing-boom-boom.

Around him so many danced and howled
That none could him espy.
You could only see him from above
Where stars looked down from the sky.

Not always do the stars remain:
There comes a dawn at length.
Yet the soldier as he was taught
Pursued his hero's death.

GROSSER DANKCHORAL

Lobet die Nacht und die Finsternis, die euch umfangen!
Kommet zuhauf
Schaut in den Himmel hinauf:
Schon ist der Tag euch vergangen.

Lobet das Gras und die Tiere, die neben euch leben und sterben!
Sehet, wie ihr
Lebet das Gras und das Tier
Und es muss auch mit euch sterben.

Lobet den Baum, der aus Aas aufwächst jauchzend zum Himmel!
Lobet das Aas
Lobet den Baum, der es frass
Aber auch lobet den Himmel.

Lobet von Hertzen das schlechte Gedächtnis des Himmels!
Und das ser nicht
Weiss euren Nam' noch Gesicht
Niemand weiss, dass ihr noch da seid.

Lobet die Kälte, die Finsternis und das Verderben!
Schauet hinan:
Es kommet nicht auf euch an
Und ihr könnt unbesorgt sterben.

GRAND CHORALE OF THANKSGIVING

Praise ye the night and the darkness which surround you!
Gather in crowds,
Look into the heavens above you,
Already the day fleeth from you.

Praise ye the grass and the beast which neighbor you, living and
    dying.
Behold, like to yours
Is the life of the grass and the beast,
Like to yours must be their dying.

Praise ye the tree which groweth exultant from carrion unto heaven!
Praise ye carrion,
Praise ye the tree that ate of it
But praise ye the heavens likewise.

Praise ye from your hearts the unmindfulness of heaven!
Since it knoweth not
Either your name or your face,
No one knoweth if you are still there.

Praise ye the cold, the darkness and corruption!
Look beyond:
It heedeth you not one jot.
Unmoved, you may do your dying.

From

THE THEATER

DIE SEERÄUBER-JENNY

Meine Herren, heute sehen Sie mich Gläser abwaschen
Und ich mache das Bett für jeden.
Und Sie geben mir einen Penny, und ich bedanke mich schnell
Und Sie sehen meine Lumpen und dies lumpige Hotel
Und Sie wissen nicht, mit wem Sie reden.
Aber eines Abends wird ein Geschrei sein am Hafen
Und man fragt: Was ist das für ein Geschrei?
Und man wird mich lächeln sehn bei meinen Gläsern
Und man sagt: Was lächelt die dabei?
      Und ein Schiff mit acht Segeln
      Und mit fünfzig Kanonen
      Wird liegen am Kai.

Und man sagt: Geh, wisch deine Gläser, mein Kind!
Und man reicht mir den Penny hin
Und der Penny wird genommen
Und das Bett wird gemacht
Es wird keiner mehr drin schlafen in dieser Nacht
Und Sie wissen immer noch nicht, wer ich bin.
Denn an diesem Abend wird ein Getös sein am Hafen
Und man fragt: Was ist das für ein Getös?
Und man wird mich stehen sehen hinterm Fenster
Und man sagt: Was lächelt die so bös?
      Und das Schiff mit acht Segeln
      Und mit fünfzig Kanonen
      Wird beschiessen die Stadt.

Meine Herren, da wird wohl Ihr Lachen aufhören
Denn die Mauern werden fallen hin
Und die Stadt wird gemacht dem Erdboden gleich
Nur ein lumpiges Hotel wird verschont von jedem Streich
Und man fragt: Wer wohnt Besonderer darin?
Und in dieser Nacht wird ein Geschrei um das Hotel sein
Und man fragt: Warum wird das Hotel verschont?
And man wird mich sehen treten aus der Tür gen Morgen
Und man sagt: Die hat darin gewohnt?

JENNY THE PIRATE

Good Sirs, today you see me rinsing out the glasses
And I make up the beds for all of you.
And I get penny tips and I thank the clientele
And you see me in rags in this filthy hotel
And you don't know who you're talking to.
But one fine evening there'll be screams in the harbor
And they'll ask: what can it be that we hear?
And they'll see me laughing as I wash out the glasses
And they'll say: her laughter's very queer.

        And a ship with eight sails
        And with fifty cannons
        Will tie up to the pier.

They say, go, wash your glasses my child,
And the penny they drop in my hand
And I put it in my pocket
And I pull the sheets tight
But not one of you will sleep in them tonight
And you still have no idea who I am.
But one fine evening there'll be a crash in the harbor
And they'll ask: what is that awful noise?
And they'll see me standing in front of the window
And they'll say: her laughter isn't nice.

        And the ship with eight sails
        And with fifty cannons
        Will bombard the city.

Good Sirs, then you'll surely stop your laughing
For the walls will fall in a minute
And the town will be flattened into the dust.
Just a filthy hotel will be spared as it must
And they'll ask: what special person lives in it?
All through the night there'll be shrieks where the hotel is
And they'll say: why should *this* hotel be spared?
When they see me walk out of the door toward morning
They'll say: Oh, *she* was living there?

Und das Schiff mit acht Segeln
Und mit fünfzig Kanonen
Wird beflaggen den Mast.

Und es werden kommen hundert gen Mittag an Land
Und werden in den Schatten treten
Und fangen einen jeglichen aus jeglicher Tür
Und legen ihn in Ketten und bringen vor mir
Und fragen: Welchen sollen wir töten?
Und an diesem Mittag wird es still sein am Hafen
Wenn man fragt, wer wohl sterben muss.
Und dann werden Sie mich sagen hören: Alle!
Und wenn dann der Kopf fällt, sag ich: Hoppla!
Und das Schiff mit acht Segeln
Und mit fünfzig Kanonen
Wird entschwinden mit mir.

—Die Dreigroschenoper

68

And the ship with eight sails
And with fifty cannons
Will run flags up the mast.

And a hundred men toward midday will all come ashore
And march by the shadowy water
And quickly haul everyone into the street
And put them in irons and lay them at my feet
And they'll ask me: which ones shall we slaughter?
And the harbor will be silent on this midday
When they ask: now who shall it be?
And then you'll hear me cry aloud: all of them!
And with each head that falls I'll shout: hurray!
And the ship with eight sails
And with fifty cannons
Will vanish with me.

DAS LIED VON DER UNZULÄNGLICHKEIT MENSCHLICHEN STREBENS

Der Mensch lebt durch den Kopf
Der Kopf reicht ihm nicht aus
Versuch es nur, von deinem Kopf
Lebt höchstens eine Laus.
   Denn für dieses Leben
   Ist der Mensch nicht schlau genug
   Niemals merkt er eben
   Allen Lug und Trug.

Ja, mach nur einen Plan
Sei nur ein grosses Licht!
Und mach dann noch 'nen zweiten Plan
Gehn tun sie beide nicht.
   Denn für dieses Leben
   Ist der Mensch nicht schlecht genug
   Doch sein höh'res Streben
   Ist ein schöner Zug.

Ja, renn nur nach dem Glück
Doch renne nicht zu sehr!
Denn all rennen nach dem Glück
Das Glück rennt hinterher.
   Denn für dieses Leben
   Ist der Mensch nicht anspruchlos genug
   Drum ist all sein Streben
   Nur ein Selbstbetrug.

Der Mensch ist gar nicht gut
Drum hau ihn auf den Hut.
Hast du ihn auf den Hut gehaut
Dann wird er vielleicht gut.
   Denn für dieses Leben
   Ist der Mensch nicht gut genug
   Darum haut ihn eben
   Ruhig auf den Hut.

      —DIE DREIGROSCHENOPER

SONG OF THE INADEQUACY OF MAN'S HIGHER NATURE

A man lives by his head:
His head will not suffice.
Just take a look at your own heads
At most supporting lice.
        For this world we live in
        None of us is sly enough.
        Never do we notice
        All is lie and bluff.

Make yourself a plan,
One that dazzles you!
Now make yourself a second plan,
Neither one will do.
        For this world we live in
        None of us is bad enough.
        Yet our higher nature's
        Made of splendid stuff.

Chase after luck and joy
Yet running will not find them!
For all men chase and luck and joy
Are running just behind them.
        For this world we live in
        None of us has modesty enough.
        Thus our higher nature
        Is but pose and bluff.

Man is not good at all
So boot him in the can.
Perhaps if he's kicked soundly
He'll be a better man.
        For this world we live in
        None of us is good enough
        Therefore let us calmly
        Boot each other's can.

SALOMON-SONG

Ihr saht den weisen Salomon
Ihr wisst, was aus ihm wurd.
Dem Mann war alles sonnenklar
Er verfluchte die Stunde seiner Geburt
Und sah, das alles eitel war.
Wie gross und weis war Salomon!
Und seht, da war es noch nicht Nacht
Da sah die Welt die Folgen schon:
Die Weisheit hatte ihn so weit gebracht—
Beneidenswert, wer frei davon!

Ihr saht die schöne Kleopatra
Ihr wisst, was aus ihr wurd!
Zwei Kaiser fielen ihr zum Raub
Da hat sie sich zu Tod gehurt
Und welkte hin und wurde Staub.
Wie schön und gross war Babylon!
Und seht, da war es noch nicht Nacht
Da sah die Welt die Folgen schon:
Die Schönheit hatte sie so weit gebracht—
Beneidenswert, wer frei davon!

Ihr saht den kühnen Cäsar dann
Ihr wisst, was aus ihm wurd!
Der sass wie 'n Gott auf 'nem Altar
Und wurde ermordet, wie ihr erfuhrt
Und zwar, als er am grössten war.
Wie schrie der laut „Auch du, mein Sohn!"
Und seht, da war es noch nicht Nacht
Da sah die Welt die Folgen schon:
Die Kühnheit hatte ihn so weit gebracht—
Beneidenswert, wer frei davon!

Ihr kennt den wissensdurstigen Brecht
Ihr sangt ihn allesamt.
Dann hat er euch zu oft gefragt
Woher der Reichen Reichtum stammt

SOLOMON SONG

Behold wise Solomon, mark well
The sorry fate that him befell!
All things were clear to him as dawn.
He cursed the day that he was born
And saw that all was vanity.
How great and wise a man was he!
Behold, before the day was done
The truth was clear to everyone:
Since wisdom brought him his sad end
The fellow's lucky who has none.

Fair Cleopatra now mark well,
The sorry fate that her befell!
She snared two Caesars for her prey
And yet she whored her life away
And withered and was turned to dust.
How fair was Babylon in the past!
Behold, before the day was done
The truth was plain to everyone:
Since beauty brought her her sad end
The woman's lucky who has none.

Behold brave Caesar and mark well
The sorry fate that him befell!
Godlike he sat upon his throne—
His cruel murder is well known
Just when his greatness had begun.
How loud he cried, "You, too, my son!"
Behold before the day was done
The truth was plain to everyone:
Since bravery brought him his sad end
The fellow's lucky who has none.

And now the studious Brecht mark well,
Whose songs you sang, I have heard tell.
Too often to preserve his health
He asked where rich men got their wealth.

Da habt ihr ihn jäh aus dem Land gejagt.
Wie wissensdurstig war doch meiner Mutter Sohn!
Und sieh, da war es noch nicht Nacht
Da sah die Welt die Folgen schon:
Sein Wissensdurst hat ihn soweit gebracht—
Beneidenswert, wer frei davon!

Und jetzt seht ihr den Herrn Macheath
Sein kopf hängt an 'nem Haar!
Solang er folgte der Vernunft
Und raubte, was zu rauben war
War er ein Grosser in seiner Zunft.
Dann lief sein Herz mit ihm davon!
Und seht, jetzt ist es noch nicht Nacht
Da sieht die Welt die Folgen schon:
Die Sinnlichkeit hat ihn so weit gebracht—
Beneidenswert, wer frei davon!

—DIE DREIGROSCHENOPER

74

Then from your land he had to run,
How studious was my mother's son!
Behold before the day was done
The truth was plain to everyone:
Since knowledge brought him his sad end
The fellow's lucky who has none.

Behold Macheath whose comely head
Just now is dangling by a thread!
For, while he followed reason's rule
And stole whate'er there was to steal,
He was a great man in his trade
Then by his heart he was betrayed!
Behold, before the day is done
The truth is plain to everyone:
A lustful heart brought his sad end
The fellow's lucky who has none.

JENNY-SONG

Meine Herren, meine Mutter prägte
Auf mich einst ein schlimmes Wort:
Ich würde enden im Schauhaus
Oder an einem noch schlimmern Ort.
Ja, so ein Wort, das ist leicht gesagt.
Aber ich sage euch: daraus wird nichts!
Das könnt ihr nicht machen mit mir!
Was aus mir noch wird, das werden wir sehen!
Ein Mensch ist kein Tier!
Denn wie man sich bettet, so liegt man
Es deckt einen keiner da zu
Und wenn einer tritt, dann bin ich es
Und wird einer getreten, dann bist's du.

Meine Herren, mein Freund, der sagte
Mir damals ins Gesicht:
„Das Grösste auf Erden ist Liebe"
Und „An morgen denkt man nicht."
Ja, Liebe, das ist leicht gesagt;
Doch solang man täglich älter wird
Da wird nicht nach Liebe gefragt
Da muss man seine kurze Zeit benützen.
Ein Mensch ist kein Tier!
Denn wie man sich bettet, so liegt man
Es deckt einen keiner da zu
Und wenn einer tritt, dann bin ich es
Und wird einer getreten, dann bist's du.

—Aufstieg und Fall der Stadt Mahagonny

JENNY'S SONG

Good Sirs, my mother once shouted
A nasty word in my face:
She said I'd end in the morgue
Or perhaps in a still worse place.
Yes, it's very easy to talk
But I say don't give it a thought!
I won't fall for that in the least!
Just wait and see what becomes of a girl like me!
A person's not a beast!
As you make your bed you must lie
And no one denies it's true
And if anyone does any stepping, that's me,
And when anyone's stepped on, that's you.

Good Sirs, I had a friend once
Who always used to say,
"Love is the greatest thing on earth,"
And, "Let's just think of today."
Yes, Darling, that's easily said,
But when you aren't young any more
All of life isn't lived in bed.
When you haven't much time you have to make use of it.
A person's not a beast!
As you make your bed you must lie
And no one denies it's true.
And if anyone does any stepping, that's me,
And when anyone's stepped on, that's you.

GOTT IN MAHAGONNY

An einem grauen Vormittag
Mitten im Whisky
Kam Gott nach Mahagonny.
Mitten im Whisky
Bemerkten wir Gott in Mahagonny.

Sauft ihr wie die Schwämme
Meinen guten Weizen Jahr für Jahr?
Keiner hat erwartet, dass ich käme
Wenn ich komme jetzt, ist alles gar?
Ansahen sich die Männer von Mahagonny.
Ja, sagten die Männer von Mahagonny.

An einem grauen Vormittag
Mitten im Whisky
Kam Gott nach Mahagonny.
Mitten im Whisky
Bemerkten wir Gott in Mahagonny.

Lachet ihr am Freitag abend?
Mary Weeman sah ich ganz von fern
Wie 'nen Stockfisch stumm im Salzsee schwimmen
Sie wird nicht mehr trocken, meine Herrn.
Ansahen sich die Männer von Mahagonny.
Ja, sagten die Männer von Mahagonny.

An einem grauen Vormittag
Mitten im Whisky
Kam Gott nach Mahagonny.
Mitten im Whisky
Bemerkten wir Gott in Mahagonny.

Kennt ihr diese Patronen?
Schiesst ihr meinen guten Missionar?
Soll ich wohl mit euch im Himmel wohnen?
Sehen euer graues Säuferhaar?
Ansahen sich die Männer von Mahagonny.
Ja, sagten die Männer von Mahagonny.

GOD IN MAHAGONNY

On a somber forenoon
In the midst of the whiskey
God came to Mahagonny.
In the midst of the whiskey
We noticed God in Mahagonny.

Like sponges have you soaked up
My good rye from year to year?
No one awaited my coming,
Are you all ready now I'm here?
They looked at each other, the men of Mahagonny.
Yes, answered the men of Mahagonny.

On a somber forenoon
In the midst of the whiskey
God came to Mahagonny.
In the midst of the whiskey
We noticed God in Mahagonny.

While you laughed on Friday evening
I saw Mary Weeman, Gentlemen,
Float mute as a dried cod in the ocean
And she'll never be dry again.
They looked at each other, the men of Mahagonny.
Yes, answered the men of Mahagonny.

On a somber forenoon
In the midst of the whiskey
God came to Mahagonny.
In the midst of the whiskey
We noticed God in Mahagonny.

Do you know these fellows here?
Was it my good preacher that you shot?
Must I dwell in heaven with you,
Look upon such gray-haired sots?
They looked at each other, the men of Mahagonny.
Yes, answered the men of Mahagonny.

An einem grauen Vormittag
Mitten im Whisky
Kam Gott nach Mahagonny.
Mitten im Whisky
Bemerkten wir Gott in Mahagonny.

Gehet alle zur Hölle!
Steckt jetzt die Virginien in den Sack!
Marsch mit euch in meine Hölle, Burschen!
In die schwarze Hölle mit euch Pack!
Ansahen sich die Männer von Mahagonny.
Ja, sagten die Männer von Mahagonny.

An einem grauen Vormittag
Mitten im Whisky
Kommst du nach Mahagonny.
Mitten im Whisky
Fängst an du in Mahagonny!

Rühre keiner den Fuss jetzt!
Jedermann streikt! An den Haaren
Kannst du uns nicht in die Hölle ziehen:
Weil wir immer in der Hölle waren.
Ansahen Gott die Männer von Mahagonny.
Nein, sagten die Männer von Mahagonny.

—AUFSTIEG UND FALL DER STADT MAHAGONNY

On a somber forenoon
In the midst of the whiskey
God came to Mahagonny.
In the midst of the whiskey
We noticed God in Mahagonny.

Off you go to hell!
Put your cigarettes away!
Forward march into my hell, boys,
Into hell and no delay!
They looked at each other, the men of Mahagonny.
Yes, answered the men of Mahagonny.

On a somber forenoon
In the midst of the whiskey
You come to Mahagonny.
In the midst of the whiskey
You begin in Mahagonny!
Let nobody move an inch.

We're on strike. Keep calm, steady!
You can't drag us off to hell
When we live in hell already.
They looked at God, the men of Mahagonny.
No, answered the men of Mahagonny.

LIED VON DER BELEBENDEN WIRKUNG DES GELDES

Niedrig gilt das Geld auf dieser Erden
Und doch ist sie, wenn es mangelt, kalt
Und sie kann sehr gastlich werden
Plötzlich durch des Gelds Gewalt.
Eben war noch alles voll Beschwerden
Jetzt ist alles golden überhaucht
Was gefroren hat, das sonnt sich
Jeder hat das, was er braucht.
Rosig färbt der Horizont sich
Blicket hinan: der Schornstein raucht!
Ja, das schaut sich alles gleich ganz anders an.
Voller schlägt das Herz. Der Blick wird weiter.
Reichlich ist das Mahl. Flott sind die Kleider.
Und der Mann ist jetzt ein andrer Mann.

Ach, sie gehen alle in die Irre
Die da glauben, dass am Geld nichts liegt.
Aus der Fruchbarkeit wird Dürre
Wenn der gute Strom versiegt.
Jeder schreit nach was und nimmt es, wo er's kriegt.
Eben war noch alles nicht so schwer.
Wer nicht grade Hunger hat, verträgt sich
Jetzt ist alles herz-und liebeleer.
Vater, Mutter, Brüder: alles schlägt sich!
Sehet, der Schornstein, er raucht nicht mehr!
Überall dicke Luft, die uns gar nicht gefällt.
Alles voller Hass und voller Neider.
Keiner will mehr Pferd sein, jeder Reiter
Und die Welt ist eine kalte Welt.

So ist's auch mit allem Guten und Grossen.
Es verkümmert rasch in dieser Welt
Denn mit leerem Magen und mit blossen
Füssen ist man nicht auf Grösse eingestellt.
Man will nicht das Gute, sondern Geld

SONG OF THE INVIGORATING EFFECT OF MONEY

Upon this earth we hear dispraise of money
Yet, without it, earth is very cold
And it can be warm and friendly
Suddenly through the power of gold.
Everything that seemed so hard to bear
In a gleaming golden glow is cloaked.
Sun is melting what was frozen.
Every man fulfills his hopes!
Rosy beams light the horizon,
Look on high: the chimney smokes!
Yes, all at once this world seems quite a different one.
Higher beats the heart, the glance sweeps wider.
Richer are the meals and clothes are finer.
Man himself becomes another man.

Ah, how very sorely they're mistaken,
They who think that money doesn't count.
Fruitfulness turns into famine
When the kindly stream gives out.
Each one starts to yell and grabs it where he can.
Even were it not so hard to live
He who doesn't hunger yet is fearful.
Every heart is empty now of love.
Father, Mother, Brother—cross and tearful!
See, the chimney smokes no more above!
Thick displeasing fog about us furled,
All is filled with hatred now and striving.
None will be the horse, all would be riding
And the world becomes an icy world.

So it goes with all that's great and worthy.
In this world it's quickly spoiled indeed,
For when feet are bare and bellies empty
Love of virtue always turns to greed.
Gold, not greatness, is what people need.

Und man ist von Kleinmut angehaucht.
Aber wenn der Gute etwas Geld hat
Hat er, was er doch zum Gutsein braucht.
Wer sich schon auf Untat eingestellt hat
Blicke hinan: der Schornstein raucht!
Ja, da glaubt man wieder an das menschliche Geschlecht.
Edel sei der Mensch, gut und so weiter.
Die Gesinnung wächst. Sie war geschwächt.
Fester wird das Herz. Der Blick wird breiter.
Man erkennt, was Pferd ist und was Reiter.
Und so wird das Recht erst wieder Recht.

—DIE RUNDKÖPFE UND DIE SPITZKÖPFE

Poverty of soul puts out our hopes.
Good plus money, too, is what it takes
To keep man virtuous without a slip.
He whom crime's already given breaks
Looks up on high: the chimney smokes!
Faith in the human race again grows bright.
Man is noble, good, so on and so forth.
Sentiment awakes. Need dimmed its light.
Faster beats the heart. The glance sweeps wider.
We know who the horse is, who the rider.
And once more it's clear that right is right.

NANNAS LIED

Meine Herrn, mit siebzehn Jahren
Kam ich auf den Liebesmarkt
Und ich habe viel erfahren.
Böses gab es viel
Doch das war das Spiel.
Aber manches hab ich doch verargt.
(Schliesslich bin ich auch nur ein Mensch.)
Gottseidank geht alles schnell vorüber
Auch die Liebe und der Kummer sogar.
Wo sind die Tränen von gestern Abend?
Wo ist der Schnee vom vergangenen Jahr?

Freilich geht man mit den Jahren
Leichter auf den Liebesmarkt
Und umarmt sie dort in Scharen.
Aber das Gefühl
Wird erstaunlich kühl
Wenn man damit allzuwenig kargt.
(Schliesslich geht ja jeder Vorrat zu Ende.)
Gottseidank geht alles schnell vorüber
Auch die Liebe und der Kummer sogar.
Wo sind die Tränen von gestern Abend?
Wo ist der Schnee vom vergangenen Jahr?

Und auch wenn man gut das Handeln
Lernte auf der Liebesmess':
Lust in Kleingeld zu verwandeln
Wird doch niemals leicht.
Nun, es wird erreicht.
Doch man wird auch älter unterdes.
(Schliesslich bleibt man ja auch nicht immer siebzehn.)
Gottseidank geht alles schnell vorüber
Auch die Liebe und der Kummer sogar.
Wo sind die Tränen von gestern abend?
Wo ist der Schnee vom vergangenen Jahr?

—DIE RUNDKÖPFE UND DIE SPITZKÖPFE

NANNA'S SONG

Good Sirs, at seventeen summers
I went to Lechery Fair
And plenty of things it's taught me.
Many a heartache,
That's the chance you take.
But I've wept many times in despair.
(After all I'm a human being, too.)
Thank God it's all over with quickly,
All the love and the grief we must bear.
Where are the tears of yesterevening?
Where are the snows of yesteryear?

As the years pass by it gets easy,
Easy in Lechery Fair.
And you fill your arms with so many.
But tenderness
Grows strangely less
When you spend with so little care.
(For every stock runs out in the end.)
Thank God it's all over with quickly,
All the love and the grief we must bear.
Where are the tears of yesterevening?
Where are the snows of yesteryear?

And, though you may learn your trade well,
Learn it at Lechery Fair,
Bartering lust for small change
Is a hard thing to do.
Well, it comes to you.
But you don't grow younger there.
(After all you can't stay seventeen forever.)
Thank God it's all over with quickly,
All the love and the grief we must bear.
Where are the tears of yesterevening?
Where are the snows of yesteryear?

DAS LIED VOM WASSERRAD

Von den Grossen dieser Erde
Melden uns die Heldenlieder:
Steigend auf so wie Gestirne
Gehn sie wie Gestirne nieder.
Das klingt tröstlich und man muss es wissen.
Nur: für uns, die sie ernähren müssen
Ist das leider immer ziemlich gleich gewesen.
Aufstieg oder Fall: wer trägt die Spesen?
      Freilich dreht das Rad sich immer weiter
      Dass, was oben ist, nicht oben bleibt.
      Aber für das Wasser unten heisst das leider
      Nur: dass es das Rad halt ewig treibt.

Ach, wir hatten viele Herren
Hatten Tiger und Hyänen
Hatten Adler, hatten Schweine
Doch wir nährten den und jenen.
Ob sie besser waren oder schlimmer:
Ach, der Stiefel glich dem Stiefel immer
Und uns trat er. Ihr versteht, ich meine
Dass wir keine andern Herren brauchen, sondern keine!
      Freilich dreht das Rad sich immer weiter
      Dass, was oben ist, nicht oben bleibt.
      Aber für das Wasser unten heisst das leider
      Nur: dass es das Rad halt ewig treibt.

Und sie schlagen sich die Köpfe blutig
Raufend um die Beute
Nennen andre gierige Tröpfe
Und sich selber gute Leute.
Unaufhörlich sehn wir sie einander grollen
Und bekämpfen. Einzig und alleinig
Wenn wir sie nicht mehr ernähren wollen
Sind sie sich auf einmal völlig einig.

THE SONG OF THE WATERWHEEL

Ancient tale and epic story
Tell of heroes' lives untarnished:
Like the stars they rose in glory,
Like the stars they set when vanquished.
This is comforting and we should know it.
We, alas, who plant the wheat and grow it
Have but little share in triumphs or disasters.
Rise to fame or fall: who feeds our masters?
　　　　Yes, the wheel is always turning madly,
　　　　Neither side stays up or down,
　　　　But the water underneath fares badly
　　　　For it has to make the wheel go round.

Ah, we've had so many masters,
Swine or eagle, lean or fat one:
Some were tigers, some hyenas,
Still we fed this one and that one.
Whether one is better than the other:
Ah, one boot is always like another
When it treads upon you. What I say about them
Is we need no other masters: we can do without them!
　　　　Yes, the wheel is always turning madly,
　　　　Neither side stays up or down,
　　　　But the water underneath fares badly
　　　　For it has to make the wheel go round.

And they beat each other's heads all bloody
Scuffling over booty,
Call the other fellows greedy wretches,
They, themselves, but do their duty.
Ceaselessly we see their wars grow grimmer,
Would I knew a way for them to be united.
If we will no more provide the fodder
Maybe that's the way all could be righted.

Denn dann dreht das Rad sich nicht mehr weiter
Und dies grosse Reiten unterbleibt
Wenn das Wasser sich dem Wasser eint und heiter
Endlich einmal nur sich selber treibt.

—DIE RUNDKÖPFE UND DIE SPITZKÖPFE

For at last the wheel shall turn no longer,
And shall ride the stream no more,
When the water joins to water as it gaily
Drives itself, freed of the load it bore.

LOB DES LERNENS

Lerne das Einfachste! Für die
deren Zeit gekommen ist
ist es nie zu spät!
Lerne das ABC, es genügt nicht, aber
lerne es! Lass es dich nicht verdriessen!
fang an! Du musst alles wissen!
Du musst die Führung übernehmen!

Lerne, Mann im Asyl!
Lerne, Mann im Gefängnis!
Lerne, Frau in der Küche!
Lerne, Sechzigjährige!
Suche die Schule auf, Obdachloser!
Verschaffe dir Wissen, Frierender!
Hungriger, greif nach dem Buch: es ist ein Waffe.
Du musst die Führung übernehmen.

Scheu dich nicht zu fragen, Genosse!
Lass dir nichts einreden
sieh selber nach!
Was du nicht selber weisst
weisst du nicht.
Prüfe die Rechnung.
Du musst sie bezahlen.
Lege den Finger auf jeden Posten
frage: wie kommt er hierher?
Du musst die Führung übernehmen.

—Die Mutter

PRAISE OF LEARNING

Learn the simplest things. For you
whose time has already come
it is never too late!
Learn your A B C's, it is not enough,
but learn them! Do not let it discourage you,
begin! You must know everything!
You must take over the leadership!

Learn, man in the asylum!
Learn, man in prison!
Learn, wife in the kitchen!
Learn, man of sixty!
Seek out the school, you who are homeless!
Sharpen your wits, you who shiver!
Hungry man, reach for the book: it is a weapon.
You must take over the leadership.

Don't be afraid of asking, brother!
Don't be won over,
see for yourself!
What you don't know yourself,
you don't know.
Add up the reckoning.
It's you who must pay it.
Put your finger on each item,
ask: how did this get here?
You must take over the leadership.

LIED VOM FLICKEN UND VOM ROCK

Immer, wenn unser Rock zerfetzt ist
kommt ihr gelaufen und sagt: so geht das nicht weiter!
dem muss abgeholfen werden und mit allen Mitteln!
Und voll Eifer rennt ihr zu den Herren
während wir, stark frierend, warten.
Und ihr kehrt zurück und im Triumphe
zeigt ihr uns, was ihr für uns erobert:
einen kleinen Flicken.
                    Gut, das ist der Flicken.
                    Aber wo ist
                    der ganze Rock?

Immer, wenn wir vor Hunger schreien
kommt ihr gelaufen und sagt: so geht das nicht weiter!
dem muss abgeholfen werden und mit allen Mitteln!
Und voll Eifer rennt ihr zu den Herren
während wir, voll Hunger, warten.
Und ihr kehrt zurück und im Triumphe
zeigt ihr uns, was ihr für uns erobert:
ein Stücklein Brot.
                    Gut, das ist das Stücklein Brot.
                    Aber wo ist
                    der Brotlaib?

Wir brauchen nicht nur den Flicken
Wir brauchen den ganzen Rock
wir brauchen nicht nur das Stück Brot
wir brauchen den Brotlaib selbst.
Wir brauchen nicht nur den Arbeitsplatz
wir brauchen die ganze Fabrik und die Kohle und das Erz und
die Macht im Staat.
                    Gut, das ist, was wir brauchen.
                    Aber was
                    bietet ihr uns an?

—DIE MUTTER

SONG OF THE PATCH
AND THE OVERCOAT

Whenever our overcoat is ragged
you come running up and say: this can't continue,
you must be helped in every possible manner.
And, full of zeal, you run off to the bosses
while we who freeze are waiting.
And you come back and in triumph
show us what you have won for us:
a little patch.

> Fine, that's a patch all right
> but where is
> the whole coat?

Whenever we cry aloud from hunger
you come running up and say: this can't continue,
you must be helped in every possible manner.
And, full of zeal, you run to the bosses
while we who starve are waiting.
And you come back and in triumph
show us what you have won for us,
a crumb of bread.

> Fine, that's the breadcrumb
> but where is
> the whole loaf?

We need much more than patches,
we need the whole overcoat, too;
we need much more than the breadcrumb,
we need the loaf itself.
We need much more than a job,
we need the whole factory and the coal and the ore and
power in the state.

> Fine, that's what we all need
> but what
> do you offer us?

GESANG DER REISKAHNSCHLEPPER

In der Stadt oben am Fluss
gibt es für uns einen Mundvoll Reis
aber der Kahn ist schwer, der hinauf soll
und das Wasser fliesst nach unten
wir werden nie hinaufkommen.
> Zieht rascher, die Mäuler
> warten auf das Essen.
> Zieht gleichmässig. Stosst nicht
> den Nebenmann.

Die Nacht kommt schon bald. Das Lager
zu klein für eines Hundes Schatten
kostet einen Mundvoll Reis.
Weil das Ufer zu glatt ist
kommen wir nicht vom Fleck.
> Zieht rascher, die Mäuler
> warten auf das Essen.
> Zieht gleichmässig. Stosst nicht
> den Nebenmann.

Länger als wir
hält das Tau, das in die Schultern schneidet.
Die Peitsche des Aufsehers
hat vier Geschlechter gesehen
wir sind nicht das letzte.
> Zieht rascher, die Mäuler
> warten auf das Essen.
> Zieht gleichmässig. Stosst nicht
> den Nebenmann.

Unsere Väter zogen den Kahn von der Flussmündung
ein Stück weit höher. Unsere Kinder
werden die Quelle erreichen, wir
sind dazwischen.
> Zieht rascher. Die Mäuler
> warten auf das Essen.
> Zieht gleichmässig. Stosst nicht
> den Nebenmann.

SONG OF THE RICEBARGE COOLIE

In the city upstream
there is a mouthful of rice for us
but the barge that must go up is heavy
and the water flows downward;
we shall never get there.

>   Pull harder, our bellies
>   are waiting for victuals,
>   pull evenly, don't jostle
>   your neighbor.

Night will soon come. Shelter,
too little for a dog's shadow,
costs us a mouthful of rice.
Since the shore is too slippery
we do not move from the spot.

>   Pull harder, our bellies
>   are waiting for victuals,
>   pull evenly, don't jostle
>   your neighbor.

Longer than we
will the strap endure that cuts our shoulders.
The whip of the overseer
has seen four generations,
we shall not be the last one.

>   Pull harder, our bellies
>   are waiting for victuals,
>   pull evenly, don't jostle
>   your neighbor.

Our fathers hauled the barge from the river mouth,
only a short distance. Our children
shall reach the source but we
are between them.

>   Pull harder, our bellies
>   are waiting for victuals,
>   pull evenly, don't jostle
>   your neighbor.

Im Kahn ist Reis. Der Bauer, der
ihn geerntet hat, bekam
eine Handvoll Münzen, wir
kriegen noch weniger. Ein Ochse
wäre teurer. Wir sind zu viele.
>   *Zieht rascher. Die Mäuler*
>   *warten auf das Essen.*
>   *Zieht gleichmässig. Stosst nicht*
>   *den Nebenmann.*

Wenn der Reis in der Stadt ankommt
und die Kinder fragen, wer
den schweren Kahn geschleppt hat, heisst es:
er ist geschleppt worden.
>   *Zieht rascher. Die Mäuler*
>   *warten auf das Essen.*
>   *Zieht gleichmässig. Stosst nicht*
>   *den Nebenmann.*

Das Essen von unten kommt
zu den Essern oben. Die
es schleppen, haben
nicht gegessen.

—DIE MASSNAHME

There is rice in the barge. The farmer
who harvested it received
a handful of coins, we
receive still less. An ox even
is worth more. There are too many of us.

> Pull harder, our bellies
> are waiting for victuals,
> pull evenly, don't jostle
> your neighbor.

When the rice reaches the city
and the children ask who
hauled the heavy barge, they tell them
it was hauled.

> Pull harder, our bellies
> are waiting for victuals,
> pull evenly, don't jostle
> your neighbor.

From downstream comes the rice
to the eaters above. Those
who haul it have
not eaten.

From

LIEDER, GEDICHTE UND CHÖRE;
SVENDBORGER GEDICHTE;
and unpublished poems

KEINER ODER ALLE

Sklave, wer wird dich befreien?
Die in tiefster Tiefe stehen
Werden, Kamerad, dich sehen
Und sie werden hör'n dein Schreien.
Sklaven werden dich befreien.
        Keiner oder alle. Alles oder nichts.
        Einer kann sich da nicht retten.
        Gewehre oder Ketten.
        Keiner oder alle. Alles oder nichts.

Hungernder, wer wird dich speisen?
Willst du dir ein Brot abschneiden
Komm zu uns, die Hunger leiden.
Lass uns dir die Wege weisen.
Hungernde werden dich speisen.
        Keiner oder alle. Alles oder nichts.
        Einer kann sich da nicht retten.
        Gewehre oder Ketten.
        Keiner oder alle. Alles oder nichts.

Wer, Geschlagener, wird dich rächen?
Du, dem sie den Schlag versetzten
Reih dich ein bei den Verletzten
Wir in allen unsern Schwächen
Werden, Kamerad, dich rächen.
        Keiner oder alle. Alles oder nichts.
        Einer kann sich da nicht retten.
        Gewehre oder Ketten.
        Keiner oder alle. Alles oder nichts.

Wer, Verlorener, wird es wagen?
Wer sein Elend nicht mehr tragen
Kann, muss sich zu jenen schlagen
Die aus Not schon dafür sorgen
Dass es heut heisst und nicht morgen.

ALL OF US OR NONE

Slave, who is it who shall free you?
Those in deepest darkness lying,
Comrade, these alone can see you,
They alone can hear you crying.
Comrade, only slaves can free you.
      Everything or nothing. All of us or none.
      One alone his lot can't better.
      Either gun or fetter.
      Everything or nothing. All of us or none.

You who hunger, who shall feed you?
If it's bread you would be carving,
Come to us, we too are starving.
Come to us and let us lead you.
Only hungry men can feed you.
      Everything or nothing. All of us or none.
      One alone his lot can't better.
      Either gun or fetter.
      Everything or nothing. All of us or none.

Beaten man, who shall avenge you?
You, on whom the blows are falling,
Hear your wounded brothers calling.
Weakness gives us strength to lend you.
Comrade, come, we shall avenge you.
      Everything or nothing. All of us or none.
      One alone his lot can't better.
      Either gun or fetter.
      Everything or nothing. All of us or none.

Who, O wretched one, shall dare it?
He who can no longer bear it
Counts the blows that arm his spirit,
Taught the time by need and sorrow,
Strikes today and not tomorrow.

Keiner oder alle. Alles oder nichts.
Einer kann sich da nicht retten.
Gewehre oder Ketten.
Keiner oder alle. Alles oder nichts.

Everything or nothing. All of us or none.
One alone his lot can't better.
Either gun or fetter.
Everything or nothing. All of us or none.

KOHLEN FÜR MIKE

Ich habe gehört, dass in Ohio
Zu Beginn dieses Jahrhunderts
Ein Weib wohnte zu Bidwell,
Mary McCoy, Witwe eines Bremsers,
Mit Namen Mike McCoy, in Armut.

Aber jede Nacht von den donnernden Zügen der Wheeling Railroad
Warfen die Bremser einen Kohlenklumpen
Über die Zaunlatten in den Kartoffelgarten
Mit rauher Stimme ausrufend in Eile:
Für Mike!

Und jede Nacht, wenn
Der Kohlenklumpen für Mike
An die Rückwand der Hütte schlug
Erhob sich die Alte, kroch,
Schlaftrunken in den Rock und räumte zur Seite
Den Kohlenklumpen
Geschenk der Bremser an Mike, den Gestorbenen, aber
Nicht Vergessenen.

Sie aber erhob sich so, lange vor Morgengrauen, und räumte
Ihre Geschenke aus den Augen der Welt, damit nicht
Die Männer in Ungelegenheit kämen
Bei der Wheeling Railroad.

Dieses Gedicht ist gewidmet den Kameraden
Des Bremsers Mike McCoy
(Gestorben wegen zu schwacher Lunge
Auf den Kohlenzügen Ohios)
Für Kameradschaft.

COAL FOR MIKE

I have heard how in Ohio
At the beginning of this century
A woman lived in Bidwell,
Mary McCoy, widow of a brakeman,
By the name of Mike McCoy,
Lived in poverty.

But every night from the thundering trains of the Wheeling Railroad
The brakemen heaved some lumps of coal
Over the picket fence into the potato patch,
Shouting briefly in harsh voices:
For Mike!

And every night
As the lumps of coal for Mike
Crashed against the rear wall of the hut
The old woman arose, crept,
Drunk with sleep, into an overcoat and heaped
The lumps of coal to one side,
The lumps of coal,
Gift of the brakemen to Mike, dead
But not forgotten.

And she arose so long before daybreak and heaped
Her gifts away from the eyes of the world so that
The men would not get into trouble
With the Wheeling Railroad.

This poem is dedicated to the comrades
Of the brakeman Mike McCoy
(Died from a weakness of the lungs
On an Ohio coal train)
For comradeship.

FRAGEN EINES LESENDEN ARBEITERS

Wer baute das siebentorige Theben?
In den Büchern stehen die Namen von Königen.
Haben die Könige die Felsbrocken herbeigeschleppt?
Und das mehrmals zerstörte Babylon,
Wer baute es so viele Male auf? In welchen Häusern
Des goldstrahlenden Lima wohnten die Bauleute?
Wohin gingen an dem Abend, wo die chinesische Mauer fertig war,
Die Maurer? Das grosse Rom
Ist voll von Triumphbögen. Wer errichtete sie? Über wen
Triumphierten die Cäsaren? Hatte das vielbesungene Byzanz
Nur Paläste für seine Bewohner? Selbst in dem sagenhaften *Atlantis*
Brüllten in der Nacht, wo das Meer es verschlang
Die Ersaufenden nach ihren Sklaven.

Der junge Alexander eroberte Indien.
Er allein?
Cäsar schlug die Gallier.
Hatte er nicht wenigstens einen Koch bei sich?
Philipp von Spanien weinte, als seine Flotte
Untergegangen war. Weinte sonst niemand?
Friedrich der Zweite siegte im Siebenjährigen Krieg. Wer
Siegte ausser ihm?

Jede Seite ein Sieg.
Wer kochte den Siegesschmaus?
Alle zehn Jahre ein grosser Mann.
Wer bezahlte die Spesen?

So viele Berichte
So viele Fragen.

A WORKER READS HISTORY

Who built the seven gates of Thebes?
The books are filled with names of kings.
Was it kings who hauled the craggy blocks of stone?
And Babylon, so many times destroyed,
Who built the city up each time? In which of Lima's houses,
That city glittering with gold, lived those who built it?
In the evening when the Chinese wall was finished
Where did the masons go? Imperial Rome
Is full of arcs of triumph. Who reared them up? Over whom
Did the Caesars triumph? Byzantium lives in song,
Were all her dwellings palaces? And even in Atlantis of the legend
The night the sea rushed in,
The drowning men still bellowed for their slaves.

Young Alexander conquered India.
He alone?
Caesar beat the Gauls.
Was there not even a cook in his army?
Philip of Spain wept as his fleet
Was sunk and destroyed. Were there no other tears?
Frederick the Great triumphed in the Seven Years War. Who
Triumphed with him?

Each page a victory,
At whose expense the victory ball?
Every ten years a great man,
Who paid the piper?

So many particulars.
So many questions.

EINHEITSFRONTLIED

Und weil der Mensch ein Mensch ist
Drum will er was zum essen, bitte sehr!
Es macht ihn ein Geschwätz nicht satt
Das schafft kein Essen her.
> Drum links, zwei, drei! Drum links, zwei, drei!
> Wo dein Platz, Genosse, ist!
> Reih dich ein in die Arbeitereinheitsfront
> Weil du auch ein Arbeiter bist.

Und weil der Mensch ein Mensch ist
Hat er Stiefel im Gesicht nicht gern.
Er will unter sich keinen Sklaven sehn
Und über sich keinen Herrn.
> Drum links, zwei, drei! Drum links, zwei, drei!
> Wo dein Platz, Genosse, ist!
> Reih dich ein in die Arbeitereinheitsfront
> Weil du auch ein Arbeiter bist.

Und weil der Prolet ein Prolet ist
Drum wird ihn kein andrer befrein.
Es kann die Befreiung der Arbeiter nur
Das Werk der Arbeiter sein.
> Drum links, zwei, drei! Drum links, zwei, drei!
> Wo dein Platz, Genosse, ist!
> Reih dich ein in die Arbeitereinheitsfront
> Weil du auch ein Arbeiter bist.

UNITED FRONT SONG

And while a man is flesh and blood
He will ask, if you please, for bread and meat
And windy words won't be enough
For words aren't good to eat.
>   Then left, two, three! Then left, two, three!
>   Comrade, here's the place for you.
>   So fall in with the workers' united front
>   For you are a worker, too.

And while a man is flesh and blood
He won't be driven till he drops.
He will want no slaves beneath his feet
And no masters up on top.
>   Then left, two, three! Then left, two, three!
>   Comrade, here's the place for you.
>   So fall in with the workers' united front
>   For you are a worker, too.

As long as there are two classes
Proletarians must agree
It's the task of none but the working class
To set the worker free.
>   Then left, two, three! Then left, two, three!
>   Comrade, here's the place for you.
>   So fall in with the workers' united front
>   For you are a worker, too.

DEUTSCHLAND

Mögen Andere von ihrer Schande
sprechen, ich spreche von der meinen.

Oh Deutschland, bleiche Mutter!
Wie sitzest du besudelt
Unter den Völkern.
Unter den Befleckten
Fällst du auf.

Von deinen Söhnen der ärmste
Liegt erschlagen.
Als sein Hunger gross war
Haben deine anderen Söhne
Die Hand gegen ihn erhoben.
Das ist ruchbar geworden.

Mit ihren so erhobenen Händen
Erhoben gegen ihren Bruder
Gehen sie jetzt frech vor dir herum
Und lachen in dein Gesicht
Das weiss man.

In deinem Hause
Wird laut gebrüllt, was Lüge ist.
Aber die Wahrheit
Muss schweigen.
Ist es so?

Warum preisen dich ringsum die Unterdrücker, aber
Die Unterdrückten beschuldigen dich?
Die Ausgebeuteten
Zeigen mit Fingern auf dich, aber
Die Ausbeuter loben das System
Das in deinem Hause ersonnen wurde!

Und dabei sehen dich alle
Den Zipfel deines Rockes verbergen, der blutig ist
Vom Blut deines
Besten Sohnes.

GERMANY

Let others speak of her shame,
I speak of my own.

O Germany, pale mother!
How soiled you are
As you sit among the peoples.
You flaunt yourself
Among the besmirched.

The poorest of your sons
Lies struck down.
When his hunger was great
Your other sons
Raised their hands against him.
This is notorious.

With their hands thus raised,
Raised against their brother,
They march insolently around you
And laugh in your face.
This is well known.

In your house
Lies are roared aloud.
But the truth
Must be silent.
Is it so?

Why do the oppressors praise you everywhere,
The oppressed accuse you?
The plundered
Point to you with their fingers, but
The plunderer praises the system
That was invented in your house!

Whereupon everyone sees you
Hiding the hem of your mantle which is bloody
With the blood
Of your best sons.

Hörend die Reden, die aus deinem Hause dringen, lacht man.
Aber wer dich sieht, der greift nach dem Messer
Wie beim Anblick einer Räuberin.

Oh Deutschland, bleiche Mutter!
Wie haben deine Söhne dich zugerichtet
Dass du unter den Völkern sitzest
Ein Gespött oder eine Furcht!

Hearing the harangues which echo from your house, men laugh.
But whoever sees you reaches for a knife
As at the approach of a robber.

O Germany, pale mother!
How have your sons arrayed you
That you sit among the peoples
A thing of scorn and fear!

DAS LIED VOM SA-MANN

Als mir der Magen knurrte, schlief ich
Vor Hunger ein.
Da hört ich sie ins Ohr mir
Deutschland erwache! schrein.

Da sah ich viele marschieren
Sie sagten: ins Dritte Reich.
Ich hatte nichts zu verlieren
Und lief mit, wohin war mir gleich.

Als ich marschierte, marschierte
Neben mir ein dicker Bauch
Und als ich „Brot und Arbeit" schrie
Da schrie der Dicke das auch.

Der Staf hatte hohe Stiefel
Ich lief mit nassen Füssen mit
Und wir marschierten beide
In gleichem Schritt und Tritt.

Ich wollte nach links marschieren
Nach rechts marschierte er
Da liess ich mich kommandieren
Und lief blind hinterher.

Und die da Hunger hatten
Marschierten matt und bleich
Zusammen mit den Satten
In irgendein drittes Reich.

Sie gaben mir einen Revolver
Und sagten: schiess auf unsern Feind!
And als ich auf ihren Feind schoss
Da war mein Bruder gemeint.

Jetzt weiss ich: drüben steht mein Bruder.
Der Hunger ists, der uns eint
Und ich marschiere, marschiere
Mit seinem und meinem Feind.

SONG OF THE STORM TROOPER

From hunger I grew drowsy
Dulled by my belly's ache.
Then someone shouted in my ear:
Germany awake!

Then I saw many marching
Toward the Third Reich, they said.
Since I had nought to lose
I followed where they led.

And as I marched, there marched
Big Belly at my side.
When I shouted "Bread and jobs,"
"Bread and jobs," he cried.

The leaders wore high boots,
I stumbled with wet feet.
Yet all of us were marching
To the selfsame beat.

I wanted to march leftward,
Squads right, the order was.
I blindly followed orders
For better or for worse.

And toward some new Third Reich,
But scarcely knowing whither,
Pale and hungry men
And well fed marched together.

They gave me a revolver
And said: now shoot our foe!
But as I fired on his ranks
I laid my brother low.

It was my brother, hunger
Made us one I know.
And I am marching, marching
With my own and my brother's foe.

So stirbt mir jetzt mein Bruder
Ich schlacht ihn selber hin
Und weiss ich doch, dass, wenn er besiegt ist
Ich selber verloren bin.

So I have lost my brother,
I wove his winding sheet.
I know now by this victory
I wrought my own defeat.

BEGRÄBNIS DES HETZERS IM ZINKSARG

Hier, in diesem Zink
Liegt ein toter Mensch
Oder seine Beine und sein Kopf
Oder noch weniger von ihm
Oder nichts, denn er war
Ein Hetzer.

Er ist erkannt worden als der Urgrund des Übels.
Verscharrt ihn. Am besten
Geht nur seine Frau mit auf den Schindanger,
Denn wer da mitgeht
Der ist auch erkannt.

Das da in dem Zink
Hat euch vielerlei verhetzt:
Zum Sattessen
Und zum Trockenwohnen
Und zum Diekinderfüttern
Und zum Aufdempfennigbestehen
Und zur Solidarität mit allen
Unterdrückten euresgleichen und
Zum Denken.

Das da in dem Zink hat gesagt
Das eines anderen Systems in der Produktion bedarf
Und das ihr, die Millionmassen der Arbeit,
Die Führung übernehmen müsst.
Vorher wird es nicht besser für euch.

Und weil das in dem Zink das gesagt hat
Darum kam es in das Zink und muss verscharrt werden
Als ein Hetzer, der euch verhetzt hat.
Und wer da vom Sattessen spricht
Und wer da von euch trocken wohnen will
Und wer da von euch auf dem pfennig besteht
Und wer da von euch seine Kinder füttern will

BURIAL OF THE AGITATOR
IN A ZINC COFFIN

Here, in this zinc coffin,
Lies a dead man,
Or else his leg and his head,
Or still less of him,
Or nothing at all since he was
An agitator.

He has been identified as the primary cause of evil.
Shove him under the earth. At most
Only his wife will accompany him to the carrion pit,
Since whoever goes with him
Is also a marked man.

What lies in the zinc coffin
Has agitated in favor of many things:
For eating-your-fill
For a-roof-over-your-head
For feeding-your-children
For holding-out-for-the-last-penny
And for solidarity with all
The oppressed who are like you
And in favor of thinking.

And what lies in the zinc coffin has said
That another economic system was necessary
And that you, the massed millions of labor,
Must take over the leadership.
Otherwise the future will hold nothing better for you.

And because what is in the zinc coffin has said this
It ended in the zinc coffin and must be shoved under the earth
As an agitator who incited you to unrest.
And whichever of you speaks of eating his fill
And whichever of you wants a roof over his head
And whichever of you holds out for the last penny
And whichever of you wants to feed his children

Und wer da denkt und sich solidarisch erklärt
Mit allen, die unterdrückt sind,
Der soll von nun an bis in Ewigkeit
In das Zink kommen wie dieser da
Als ein Hetzer und verscharrt werden.

And whichever of you thinks and proclaims his solidarity
With all who are oppressed,
He shall from now until eternity
End in the zinc coffin like this man here
As an agitator and be shoved under the earth.

DIE BÜCHERVERBRENNUNG

Als das Regime befahl, Bücher mit schädlichem Wissen
Öffentlich zu verbrennen und allenthalben
Ochsen gezwungen wurden, Karren mit Büchern
Zu den Scheiterhaufen zu ziehen, entdeckte
Ein verjagter Dichter, einer der besten, die Liste der
Verbrannten studierend, entsetzt, dass seine
Bücher vergessen waren. Er eilte zum Schreibtisch
Zornbeflügelt und schrieb einen Brief an die Machthaber.
Verbrennt mich! schrieb er mit fliegender Feder, verbrennt mich!
Tut mir das nicht an! Lasst mich nicht übrig! Habe ich nicht
Immer die Wahrheit berichtet in meinen Büchern? Und jetzt
Werd ich von euch wie ein Lügner behandelt! Ich befehle euch:
Verbrennt mich!

THE BURNING OF THE BOOKS

When the Regime ordered that books with dangerous teachings
Should be publicly burnt and everywhere
Oxen were forced to draw carts full of books
To the funeral pyre, an exiled poet,
One of the best, discovered with fury, when he studied the list
Of the burned, that his books
Had been forgotten. He rushed to his writing table
On wings of anger and wrote a letter to those in power.
Burn me, he wrote with hurrying pen, burn me!
Do not treat me in this fashion. Don't leave me out. Have I not
Always spoken the truth in my books? And now
You treat me like a liar! I order you:
Burn me!

DER JUDE, EIN UNGLÜCK
FÜR DAS VOLK

Wie die Lautsprecher des Regimes verkünden
Sind in unserem Land an allem Unglück die Juden schuld
Die sich immerfort mehrenden Missstände
Können, da die Führung sehr weise ist,
Wie sie oft betont hat,
Nur von den sich immerfort vermindernden Juden kommen.
Nur die Juden sind schuld, dass im Volk Hunger herrscht
Obwohl die grossen Grundbesitzer sich auf den Feldern zu Tode
        arbeiten
Und obwohl die Ruhrkapitäne nur die Brosamen essen, die von der
        Arbeiter Tischen fallen.
Und nur der Jude kann dahinterstecken, wenn
Für das Brot der Weizen fehlt, weil
Das Militär für seine Übungsplätze und Kasernen
Soviel Boden beschlagnahmt hat, dass er
An Umfang einer ganzen Provinz gleichkommt. Da also
Der Jude für das Volk ein Unglück ist
Kann es hiemit für das Volk nicht schwer sein
Einen Juden zu erkennen. Es braucht dazu
Weder Geburtsregister noch äussere Merkmale
—Alles dies kann ja täuschen—es braucht nur zu fragen:
Ist der oder jener Mensch ein Unglück für uns? Dann
Ist er ein Jude. Ein Unglück erkennt man
Nicht an der Nase, sondern daran, dass
Man einen Schaden hat dadurch. Es sind nicht die Nasen
Die das Unglück sind, sondern die Taten. Es braucht einer
Da doch keine besondere Nase, um
Das Volk berauben zu können, er braucht doch nur
Zum Regime zu gehören! Jeder weiss
Dass das Regime für das Volk ein Unglück ist, wenn also
Alles Unglück vom Juden kommt, muss
Das Regime vom Juden kommen. Das ist doch einleuchtend!

THE JEW, A MISFORTUNE
FOR THE PEOPLE

As the loudspeaker of the Regime asserts
That the Jews are responsible for the misfortunes of our country,
The increasingly critical condition
Must, since the leadership is very wise,
Be entirely the fault of the ever-diminishing Jews.
Only the Jews are to blame for the hunger that reigns among the
    people
Since even the great landholders are working themselves to death on
    their estates
And even the captains of industry are eating only the crumbs that
    fall from the workers' table.
And it can only be the Jew behind it
If there is lack of wheat for bread because
The military have taken over so much land
For their maneuvers and barracks that
It equals the territory of an entire province.
Since the Jew is a misfortune for the people
This makes it very easy for the people
To recognize a Jew. For this neither
A birth certificate nor external characteristics are necessary—
All these can be deceptive—it is only necessary to ask:
Is that man a misfortune for us? Then
He is a Jew. A misfortune is not to be recognized
By its nose but by the fact that
We are injured by it. Deeds not noses
Are misfortunes. No particular
Nose is necessary in order to
Rob the people, it is only necessary
To be a part of the Regime! Everyone knows
That the Regime is a misfortune for the people and since
All misfortunes are produced by Jews, it must be
That the Regime is a product of the Jews. This is highly enlightening!

AUF DER MAUER STAND MIT KREIDE:

Sie wollen den Krieg.
Der es geschrieben hat
Ist schon gefallen.

ON THE WALL IN CHALK
IS WRITTEN:

They want war.
He who wrote it
Has already fallen.

DIE DAS FLEISCH WEGNEHMEN VOM TISCH

Lehren Zufriedenheit.
Die, für die die Gabe bestimmt ist
Verlangen Opfermut.
Die Sattgefressenen sprechen zu den Hungernden
Von den grossen Zeiten, die kommen werden.
Die das Reich in den Abgrund führen
Nennen das Regieren zu schwer
Für den einfachen Mann.

THOSE WHO TAKE THE MEAT
FROM THE TABLE

Teach contentment.
Those for whom the taxes are destined
Demand sacrifice.
Those who eat their fill speak to the hungry
Of wonderful times to come.
Those who lead the country into the abyss
Call ruling too difficult
For ordinary men.

WENN DIE OBEREN
VOM FRIEDEN REDEN

Weiss das gemeine Volk
Dass es Krieg gibt.

Wenn die Oberen den Krieg verfluchen
Sind die Gestellungsbefehle schon ausgeschrieben.

WHEN THE LEADERS SPEAK OF PEACE

The common folk know
That war is coming.

When the leaders curse war
The mobilization order is already written out.

DIE TEPPICHWEBER VON KUJAN-BULAK EHREN LENIN

Oftmals wurde geehrt und ausgiebig
Der Genosse Lenin. Büsten gibt es und Standbilder.
Städte werden nach ihm benannt und Kinder.
Reden werden gehalten in vielerlei Sprachen,
Versammlungen gibt es und Demonstrationen
Von Shanghai bis Chicago, Lenin zu Ehren.
So aber ehrten ihn die
Teppichweber von Kujan-Bulak,
Kleiner Ortschaft im südlichen Turkestan:

Zwanzig Teppichweber stehn dort abends
Fiebergeschüttelt auf von dem ärmlichen Webstuhl.
Fieber geht um: die Bahnstation
Ist erfüllt von dem Summen der Stechmücken, dicker Wolke
Die sich erhebt aus dem Sumpf hinter dem alten Kamelfriedhof.
Aber die Eisenbahn, die
Alle zwei Wochen Wasser und Rauch bringt, bringt
Eines Tages die Nachricht auch
Dass der Tag der Ehrung des Genossen Lenin bevorsteht.
Und es beschliessen die Leute von Kujan-Bulak
Teppichweber, arme Leute
Dass dem Genossen Lenin auch in ihrer Ortschaft
Aufgestellt werde eine gipserne Büste.
Als aber das Geld eingesammelt wird für die Büste
Stehen sie alle
Geschüttelt vom Fieber und zahlen
Ihre mühsam erworbenen Kopeken mit fliegenden Händen.
Und der Rotarmist, Stepa Gamalew, der
Sorgsam Zählende und genau Schauende,
Sieht die Bereitschaft, Lenin zu ehren, und freut sich,
Aber er sieht auch die unsicheren Hände.
Und er macht plötzlich den Vorschlag
Mit dem Geld für die Büste Petroleum zu kaufen und
Es auf den Sumpf zu giessen hinter dem Kamelfriedhof
Von dem her die Stechmücken kommen, welche
Das Fieber erzeugen.

THE RUGWEAVERS OF KUJAN-BULAK
HONOR LENIN

Comrade Lenin has been honored
Often and plentifully. There are busts and statues.
Cities and children have been named after him.
Speeches have been given in many languages,
Meetings held, and demonstrations
From Shanghai to Chicago, in honor of Lenin.
But this is the way the rugweavers
Honored him in Kujan-Bulak,
A small community in southern Turkestan:

Twenty rugweavers live there, in the evening
As they sit on their humble weaving stools they are racked with
    fever.
Fever spreads: the railroad station
Is filled with buzzing clouds of mosquitoes
Which arise from the swamp behind the old camel yard.
But the railroad, which
Brings water and smoke every two weeks, brings
One day the news as well
That Lenin Memorial Day is coming.
And the people of Kujan-Bulak decide,
Poor weavers that they are,
That also in their community a plaster bust
Of Comrade Lenin should be set up.
But as they collect the money for the bust
They are all
Racked with fever and count
Their hard-earned kopecks with shaking hands.
And the Red Army man, Stepa Gamelev, who
Is counting carefully and paying close attention,
Sees the readiness to honor Lenin and is glad,
But he also sees the unsteady hands.
And he suddenly makes the proposal
That they buy petroleum with the money for the bust of Lenin
And pour it in the swamp behind the camel yard
From which the mosquitoes come which
Carry the fever.

So also das Fieber zu bekämpfen in Kujan-Bulak und zwar
Zu Ehren des gestorbenen, aber
Nicht zu vergessenden
Genossen Lenin.

Sie beschlossen es. An dem Tage der Ehrung trugen sie
Ihre zerbeulten Eimer, gefüllt mit dem schwarzen Petroleum,
Einer hinter dem andern
Hinaus und begossen den Sumpf damit.

So nützten sie sich, indem sie Lenin ehrten und
Ehrten ihn, indem sie sich nützten und hatten ihn
Also verstanden.

Wir haben gehört, wie die Leute von Kujan-Bulak
Lenin ehrten. Als nun am Abend
Das Petroleum gekauft und ausgegossen über dem Sumpf war
Stand ein Mann auf in der Versammlung und der verlangte
Dass eine Tafel angebracht würde an der Bahnstation
Mit dem Bericht dieses Vorgangs, enthaltend
Auch genau den geänderten Plan und den Eintausch der
Leninbüste gegen die fiebervernichtende Tonne Petroleum.
Und dies alles zu Ehren Lenins.
Und sie machten auch das noch
Und setzten die Tafel.

Thus they would both fight the fever in Kujan-Bulak and mightily
Honor the dead but
Not to be forgotten
Comrade Lenin.

They agreed to it. On Memorial Day they carried
Their battered buckets filled with black petroleum,
One after another,
And poured it over the swamp.

Thus they helped themselves while honoring Lenin and
Honored him while helping themselves and likewise
They understood him.

We have heard how the people of Kujan-Bulak
Honored Lenin. Then in the evening of the day
When the petroleum was bought and poured over the swamp
A man arose in their assembly and he wanted
A tablet set up in the railroad station
With a notice of this event, containing the details
Of both the altered plan and the exchange
Of the Lenin bust for the fever-destroying barrels of petroleum.
And all of this in honor of Lenin.
And they did this, too,
And put up the tablet.

DER SCHUH DES EMPEDOKLES

Als Empedokles, der Agrigenter
Sich die Ehrungen seiner Mitbürger erworben hatte zugleich
Mit den Gebrechen des Alters
Beschloss er zu sterben. Da er aber
Einige liebte, von denen er wieder geliebt ward
Wollte er nicht zunichte werden vor ihnen, sondern
Lieber zu Nichts.
Er lud sie zum Ausflug, nicht alle,
Einen oder den andern liess er auch weg, so in die Auswahl
Und das gesamte Unternehmen
Zufall zu mengen.
Sie bestiegen den Ätna.
Die Mühe des Steigens
Erzeugte Schweigen. Niemand vermisste
Weise Worte. Oben
Schnauften sie aus, zum gewohnten Pulse zu kommen
Beschäftigt mit Aussicht, fröhlich am Ziel zu sein.
Unbemerkt verliess sie der Lehrer.
Als sie wieder zu sprechen begannen, merkten sie
Noch nichts, erst später
Fehlte hier und da ein Wort und sie sahen sich um nach ihm.
Er aber ging da schon längst um die Bergkuppe,
Nicht so sehr eilend. Einmal
Blieb er stehen, da hörte er
Wie entfernt weit hinter der Kuppe
Das Gespräch wieder anhub. Die einzelnen Worte
Waren nicht mehr zu verstehen: das Sterben hatte begonnen.
Als er am Krater stand,
Abgewandten Gesichts, nicht wissen wollend das Weitere
Das ihn nicht mehr betraf, bückte der Alte sich langsam,
Löste sorglich den Schuh vom Fuss und warf ihn lächelnd
Ein paar Schritte seitwärts, so dass er nicht allzu bald
Gefunden würd, aber doch rechtzeitig, nämlich,
Bevor er verfault wär. Dann erst
Ging er zum Krater. Als seine Freunde
Ohne ihn und ihn suchend zurückgekehrt waren

138

THE SHOE OF EMPEDOCLES

When Empedocles of Agrigentum
Had gained the admiration of his fellow citizens along with
The infirmities of age
He decided to die. But since he loved
A certain few by whom he, in turn, was loved
He did not wish to perish in front of them, but
Rather to disappear.
He invited them to go on an excursion, not all of them,
One or another he omitted so that in the choice
And in the collective undertaking
Chance played a part.
They climbed Ætna.
The difficulty of the climb
Exacted silence. No one missed
Wise words. At the top
They stretched out to get their breath,
Busy with the view, glad to have reached their goal.
Unnoticed the teacher left them.
As they began to speak again, at first they noticed
Nothing, only later
Here and there a word was missing and they looked around for him.
But long before he had already gone to the crater,
Not hurrying very fast. Once he stood still and he heard
How far off behind the crater
The talk arose again. Individual words
Could no longer be made out: dying had begun.
As he stood at the crater,
His face turned away, wishing to know no more of what
No longer concerned him in the distance, the old man bent slowly,
Carefully slipped a shoe from one foot and, smiling,
Tossed it a few paces to one side, so that it would not
Be found too quickly but yet at the right time, that is,
Before it had rotted. Only then
Did he go to the crater. When his friends
Returned without him, having looked for him,

139

Fing durch die nächsten Wochen und Monate mählich
Jetzt sein Absterben an, so wie er's gewünscht hatte. Immer noch
Warteten einige auf ihn, während schon andere
Ihn gestorben gaben. Immer noch stellten
Einige ihre Fragen zurück bis zu seiner Wiederkehr, während schon
    andere
Selber die Lösung versuchten. Langsam wie Wolken
Sich entfernen am Himmel, unverändert, nur kleiner werdend
Weiter weichend, wenn man nicht hinsieht, entfernter
Wenn man sie wieder sucht, vielleicht schon verwechselt mit andern
So entfernte er sich aus ihrer Gewohnheit, gewöhnlicherweise.
Dann erwuchs ein Gerücht.
Er sei nicht gestorben, da er nicht sterblich gewesen sei, hiess es.
Geheimnis umgab ihn. Es wurde für möglich gehalten
Dass ausser Irdischem Anderes sei, dass der Lauf des Menschlichen
Abzuändern sei für den Einzelnen: solches Geschwätz kam auf.
Aber zu dieser Zeit wurde dann sein Schuh gefunden, der aus Leder
Der greifbare, abgetragene, der irdische! Hinterlegt für jene, die
Wenn sie nicht sehen, sogleich mit dem glauben beginnen.
Seiner Tage Ende
War so wieder natürlich. Er war wie ein anderer gestorben.

Andere wieder beschreiben den Vorgang
Anders: dieser Empedokles habe
Wirklich versucht, sich göttliche Ehren zu sichern
Und durch geheimnisvolles Entweichen, durch einen schlauen
Zeugenlosen Sturz in den Ätna die Sage begründen wollen, er
Sei nicht von menschlicher Art, den Gesetzen des Verfalls
Nicht unterworfen. Dabei dann
Habe sein Schuh ihm den Possen gespielt, in menschliche Hände zu
    fallen.
(Einige sagen sogar der Krater selber, verärgert
Über solches Beginnen, habe den Schuh des Entarteten
Einfach ausgespien.) Aber da glauben wir lieber:
Wenn er den Schuh tatsächlich nicht auszog, hätte er eher
Nur unsere Dummheit vergessen und nicht bedacht, wie wir eilends
Dunkles noch dunkler machen wollen und lieber das Ungereimte
Glauben, als suchen nach einem zureichenden Grund. Und dann hätte
    der Berg—

Gradually through the next weeks and months
His death began, as he had wished it. There were some
Who still waited for him, while others
Gave him up for dead. Some of them held
Their questions back, awaiting his return, while others
Sought the solution themselves. Slowly as the clouds
Withdraw into the sky, unchanged, only growing smaller
And more delicate while you do not look back, more distant
When you seek them again, perhaps already mixed with others,
Thus he withdrew from their ordinary affairs in the ordinary way.
Then a rumor arose.
He could not be dead, for he had been immortal, so it went.
Mystery surrounded him. It was considered possible
That there was something beyond the earthly which modified
The course of human events for the individual, this kind of babble
    arose.
But at this time his shoe was found, the leather shoe,
Tangible, worn, earthly! Left behind for those who,
When they no longer see, immediately begin to believe.
His last days
Became real once more. He had died like anyone else.

Others might have described the foregoing
Differently: this Empedocles
Had really sought to insure himself worship as a god,
And by a secret disappearance, a sly
Leap into Ætna without witnesses, to found a legend
That he was not of human stuff, not subject to the laws
Of dissolution. And in this
His shoe played a trick on him by falling into men's hands.
(Consequently some say the crater itself, angered
By such an affair, had simply spewed up the shoe
Of the corrupt one.) But we would rather believe:
If he did not really remove his shoe, he had merely
Forgotten our stupidity and not thought how we hasten
To make obscurity more obscure and prefer to believe
The absurd rather than to seek for a sufficient cause. And anyway
    the mountain

Zwar nicht empört über solche Nachlässigkeit oder gar glaubend
Jener hätte uns täuschen wollen, um göttliche Ehren zu heimsen
(Den der Berg glaubt nichts und ist mit uns nicht beschäftigt)
Aber doch eben Feuer speiend wie immer—den Schuh uns
Ausgeworfen, und so hielten die Schüler—
Schon beschäftigt, grosses Geheimnis zu wittern
Tiefe Metaphysik zu entwickeln, nur allzu beschäftigt!—
Plötzlich bekümmert den Schuh des Lehrers in Händen, den greif-
    baren
Abgetragenen, den aus Leder, den irdischen.

Certainly did not get angry over such carelessness or because
It believed the man wished to delude us into paying him divine
    honors
(For the mountain believes nothing and is not concerned with us)
But merely spewing fire as it always did it threw up the shoe
For us and so, when the scholars were busy scenting a mystery,
Developing profound metaphysics, in fact all too busy,
Suddenly they were confounded by holding the shoe of the teacher
    in their hands, the tangible shoe,
Worn, made of leather, earthly.

DER STEINFISCHER

Der grosse Fischer ist wieder erschienen. Er sitzt in seinem morschen Bot und fischt, wenn früh die erste Lampe aufflammt und wenn die letzte am Abend gelöscht wird.

Die Dorfbewohner sitzen auf dem Kies der Böschung und sehen ihm grinsend zu. Er fischt nach Heringen, aber er zieht nur Steine hoch.

Alles lacht. Die Männer schlagen sich auf die Schenkel, die Weiber halten sich die Bäuche, die Kinder springen hoch in die Luft vor Lachen.

Wenn der grosse Fischer sein brüchiges Netz hochzieht und die Steine drin findet, verbirgt er sie nicht, sondern langt weit aus mit dem braunen starken Arm, greift den Stein, hält ihn hoch und zeigt ihn den Unglücklichen.

THE STONE FISHERMAN

The big fisherman has appeared again. He sits in his rotted
boat and fishes from the time when the first lamps flare up
early in the morning until the last one is put out in the evening.

The villagers sit on the gravel of the embankment and watch him,
Grinning. He fishes for herring but he pulls up nothing but
Stones.

They all laugh. The men slap their sides, the women hold on to
their bellies, the children leap high into the air with laughter.

When the big fisherman raises his torn net high and finds the
stones in it, he does not hide them but reaches far out with his
strong brown arm, seizes the stone, holds it high and shows it
to the unlucky ones.

1939: AUS DEM REICH KOMMEN WENIG NACHRICHTEN

Der Anstreicher spricht von kommenden grossen Zeiten.
Die Wälder wachsen noch.
Die Äcker tragen noch.
Die Städte stehen noch.
Die Menschen atmen noch.

1939: LITTLE NEWS IS REPORTED FROM THE REICH

The house painter speaks of great times to come.
The woods still grow.
The fields still bear.
The cities still stand.
Men still breathe.

KINDERKREUZZUG 1939

In Polen, im Jahr Neununddreissig
war eine blutige Schlacht
die hat viele Städte und Dörfer
zu einer Wildnis gemacht.

Die Schwester verlor den Bruder
die Frau den Mann im Heer;
zwischen Feuer und Trümmerstätte
fand das Kind die Eltern nicht mehr.

Aus Polen ist nichts mehr gekommen
nicht Brief noch Zeitungsbericht
doch in den östlichen Ländern
läuft eine seltsame Geschicht'.

Schnee fiel, als man sich's erzählte
in einer östlichen Stadt
von einem Kinderkreuzzug
der in Polen begonnen hat.

Da trippelten Kinder hungernd
in Trüpplein hinab die Chausseen
und nahmen mit sich andere, die
in zerschossenen Dörfern stehn.

Sie wollten entrinnen den Schlachten
dem ganzen Nachtmahr
und eines Tages kommen
in ein Land, wo Frieden war.

Da war ein kleiner Führer
das hat sie aufgericht'.
Er hatte eine grosse Sorge:
den Weg, den wusste er nicht.

Eine Elfjährige schleppte
ein Kind von vier Jahr
hatte alles für eine Mutter
nur nicht ein Land, wo Frieden war.

CHILDREN'S CRUSADE 1939

In 'thirty-nine in Poland
There was a bloody fight
And many a town and village
Turned to waste land over night.

Sisters lost their brothers,
Wives were widowed by the war,
And in fire and desolation
Children found their kin no more.

There came no news from Poland,
Neither letter nor printed word,
But in an eastern country
A curious tale was heard.

Snow fell, as they related
In a certain eastern town
How a new crusade of children
In Poland had begun.

For all along the highways
Troops of hungry children roamed
And gathered to them others
Who stood by ruined homes.

They wished to flee the slaughter,
For the nightmare did not cease,
And some day reach a country
Where there was peace.

They had a little leader
To show them where to go.
Yet he was sorely troubled
Since the way he did not know.

A girl of ten was carrying
A little child of four.
All she lacked to be a mother
Was a country without war.

Ein kleiner Jude marschierte im Trupp
mit einem sammtenen Kragen
der war das weisseste Brot gewohnt
und hat sich gut geschlagen.

Und zwei Brüder kamen mit
die waren grosse Strategen
stürmten eine leere Bauernhütt
und räumten sie nur vor dem Regen.

Es ging ein dünner Grauer mit
hielt sich abseits in der Landschaft
und trug an einer schrecklichen Schuld:
er kam aus einer Nazigesandtschaft.

Da war unter ihnen ein Musiker
der fand eine Trommel in einem zerschossenen Dorfladen
und durfte sie nicht schlagen
das hätt sie verraten.

Und da war ein Hund
gefangen zum Schlachten
mitgenommen als Esser
weil sie's nicht übers Herz brachten.

Da war auch eine Schule
und ein kleiner Lehrer für Kaligraphie
und ein Schüler an einer zerschossenen Tankwand
lernte schreiben bis zu FRIE....

Da war auch ein Konzert
an einem lauten Winterbach
durft einer die Trommel schlagen
da ward er nicht vernommen, ach.

Da war auch eine Liebe.
Sie war zwölf, er war fünfzehn Jahr.
In einem zerschossenen Hofe
kämmte sie ihm sein Haar.

Die Liebe konnt nicht bestehen
es kam zu grosse Kält:

150

In a coat with a velvet collar
A little Jew was dressed.
He had been reared on whitest bread
But he marched on with the rest.

Two brothers, great strategists,
Planned a bold campaign.
They stormed an empty peasant hut
But had to retreat from the rain.

There was a thin and wretched boy
Who kept himself apart.
That he had been a Nazi
Was a load of guilt in his heart.

Among them was a musician
Who found a drum in a ruined store
But was afraid to beat it
Lest their enemies should hear.

They even had a dog with them
Which they had caught for food.
They could not bear to kill it
So it followed where it would.

There was a little teacher
Who taught calligraphy.
On the broken side of a tank
They learned to spell out *free*.

They even had a concert
By a noisy waterfall.
They dared to beat the drum
Since no one heard its roll.

A girl of twelve, a boy of fifteen
Had a love affair.
And in a ruined farmyard
She sat and combed his hair.

But love could not endure,
Cold wind began to blow.

wie sollen die Bäumchen blühen
wenn so viel Schnee drauf fällt?

Da war auch ein Krieg
denn es gab noch eine andre Kinderschar
und der Krieg ging nur zu Ende
weil er sinnlos war.

Doch als der Krieg noch raste
um ein zerschossenes Bahnwärterhaus
da ging, wie es heisst, der einen Partei
plötzlich das Essen aus.

Und als die andre Partei das erfuhr
da schickte sie aus einen Mann
mit einem Sack Kartoffeln, weil
man ohne Essen nicht kämpfen kann.

Da war auch ein Gericht
und brannten zwei Kerzenlichter
und war ein peinliches Verhör.
Verurteilt wurde der Richter.

Da war auch eine Hilfe
(Hilfe hat nie geschadet)
Eine Dienstmagd hat ihnen gezeigt
wie man ein Kleines badet.

Sie hatte leider nur zwei Stunden
ihnen beizubringen
musste ihrer Herrschaft
die Betten nachbringen.

Da war auch ein Begräbnis
eines Jungen mit sammtenem Kragen
der wurde von zwei Deutschen
und zwei Polen zu Grabe getragen.

Protestant, Katholik und Nazi war da
ihn der Erde einzuhändigen
und zum Schluss sprach ein kleiner Sozialist
von der Zukunft der Lebendigen.

And how can saplings bloom
When covered deep in snow?

And then they had a war
With another children's band.
At last when they saw it had no sense
The war came to an end.

Yet while their war was raging
Around a trackwalker's hut
One party came in dire straits,
Their food was eaten up.

And when the other party knew,
They did as they thought right.
They sent a bag of potatoes
For men need food to fight.

There was a trial, too,
While two lighted candles flamed.
All through the judge was ill at ease
'Twas he whom they condemned.

Some help, indeed, they had
(Help never hurts, they say),
A servant girl who bathed a babe
To show them the proper way.

Alas she only gave them
Two hours of her time
For she had to bring her mistress
The bedsheets from the line.

They had a funeral besides,
Two Poles and two Germans carried
The boy with the velvet collar
To the place where he was buried.

There were Catholics and Protestants
And Nazis at the grave.
At the end a little Socialist spoke
On the future the living have.

So gab es Glaube und Hoffnung
nur nicht Fleisch und Brot
und keiner schelt sie mir, wenn sie was stahl'n
der ihnen nicht Essen bot.

Und keiner schelt mir den armen Mann
der sie nicht zu Tische lud:
gleich ein halbes Hundert, da handelt es sich
um Mehl, nicht um Opfermut.

Findet man zwei oder sogar drei
tut man gern dafür
aber wenn es so viele sind
schliesst man seine Tür.

In einem zerschossenen Bauernhof
haben sie Mehl gefunden.
Eine Elfjährige band sich die Schürze um
und backte sieben Stunden.

Der Teig war gut gerühret
das Feuerholz gut gehackt
das Brot ist nicht aufgegangen
sie wussten nicht, wie man Brot backt.

Sie zogen vornehmlich nach Süden.
Süden ist, wo die Sonn
mittags um zwölf Uhr steht
gradaus davon.

Sie fanden zwar einen Soldaten
verwundet im Tannengries.
Sie pflegten ihn sieben Tage
damit er den Weg ihnen wies.

Er sagte ihnen: Nach Bilgoray!
Muss stark gefiebert haben
und starb ihnen weg am achten Tag.
Sie haben auch ihn begraben.

Und da gab es ja Wegweiser
wenn auch vom Schnee verweht

So there was faith and hope
But lack of bread and meat
And if they stole let no one blame
Who never bade them eat.

Let no one blame the poor man
Who never asked them in
For many have the will but have
No flour in the bin.

And if we meet with two or three
The food is gladly shared
But when there are so many
Then every door is barred.

Yet in a ruined farmyard
They found a bag of flour.
A girl of twelve tied on an apron
And baked away for hours.

The dough was kneaded well,
The firewood cut and stacked,
But no bread rose for no one knew
The way bread should be baked.

They strove to travel southward.
The south is where, 'tis said,
At high noon the sun stands
Directly overhead.

They found a wounded soldier
In a pinewood one day
And for a week they tended him
In hopes he'd know the way.

To Bilgoray, he said to them
For the fever made him rave.
Upon the eighth day he died.
They laid him in his grave.

And then they saw a signpost,
Though covered deep with snow,

nur zeigten sie nicht mehr die Richtung an
sondern waren umgedreht.

Das war nicht etwa ein grausamer Spass
sondern aus militärischen Gründen.
Ünd als sie suchten Bilgoray
konnten sie es nicht finden.

Sie standen um ihren Führer
der sah in die Schneeluft hinein
und deutete mit der kleinen Hand
und sagte: es muss dort sein.

Einmal, nachts, sahen sie ein Feuer
da gingen sie nicht hin.
Einmal rollten drei Tanks vorbei
da waren Menschen drin.

Einmal kamen sie an eine Stadt
da machten sie einen Bogen.
Bis sie daran vorüber waren
sind sie nur nachts weitergezogen.

Wo einst das südöstliche Polen war
bei starkem Schneewehn
hat man die fünfundfünfzig
zuletzt gesehn.

Wenn ich die Augen schliesse
seh ich sie wandern
von einem zerschossenen Bauerngehöft
zu einem zerschossenen andern.

Über ihnen, in den Wolken oben
seh ich andre Züge, neue, grosse!
Mühsam wandern gegen kalte Winde
Heimatlose, Richtunglose.

Suchend nach dem Land mit Frieden
ohne Donner, ohne Feuer
nicht wie das, aus dem sie kommen,
und der Zug wird ungeheuer.

'Twas turned about and pointed wrong,
But this they did not know.

And no grim joke it was but done
On military grounds.
And long they sought for Bilgoray
Which never could be found.

They stood about their leader
Who stared at the snowy sky.
He pointed with his finger,
Saying: yonder it must lie.

Once, at night, they saw a fire
But did not venture near.
And once, with crews of men inside,
They saw three tanks appear.

Once, when they reached a city,
They turned and went around.
They did not travel on by day
Till they had passed the town.

Toward what was southeast Poland,
In deeply drifting snow,
The five and fifty children
Were last seen to go.

And if I close my eyes,
I see them wander on
From one ruined barnyard
To another one.

Above them in the clouds I see
A new and greater host,
Wearily breasting the cold wind,
Homeless and lost.

Seeking for a land of peace
Without the crash and flame of war
That scars the soil from which they came,
And this host is always more.

Und er scheint mir durch den Dämmer
bald schon gar nicht mehr derselbe:
andere Gesichtlein seh ich,
spanische, französische, gelbe!

In Polen, in jenem Januar
wurde ein Hund gefangen
der hatte um seinen mageren Hals
eine Tafel aus Pappe hangen.

Darauf stand: BITTE UM HILFE!
WIR WISSEN DEN WEG NICHT MEHR.
WIR SIND FÜNFUNDFÜNFZIG,
DER HUND FÜHRT EUCH HER.

WENN IHR NICHT KOMMEN KÖNNT
JAGT IHN WEG!
SCHIESST NICHT AUF IHN
NUR ER WEISS DEN FLECK.

Die Schrift war eine Kinderhand.
Bauern haben sie gelesen.
Seitdem sind eineinhalb Jahre um.
Der Hund ist verhungert gewesen.

Now in the gloom it seems to me
They come from many other places:
In the changing clouds I see,
Spanish, French and yellow faces.

In January of that year
Poles caught a hungry dog,
Around his neck a placard hung,
'Twas tied there with a cord.

The words thereon were: PLEASE SEND HELP!
WE DON'T KNOW WHERE WE ARE.
WE ARE FIVE AND FIFTY,
THE DOG WILL LEAD YOU HERE.

AND IF YOU CANNOT COME TO US
PLEASE DRIVE HIM OUT.
DON'T SHOOT THE DOG FOR NO ONE ELSE
CAN FIND THE SPOT.

A childish hand had written
The words the peasants read.
Since that time two years have passed.
The starving dog is dead.

UND WAS BEKAM DES SOLDATEN WEIB?

Und was bekam des Soldaten Weib
Aus der alten Hauptstadt Prag?
Aus Prag bekam sie die Stöckelschuh
Einen Gruss und dazu die Stöckelschuh
Das bekam sie aus der Stadt Prag.

Und was bekam des Soldaten Weib
Aus Oslo über dem Sund?
Aus Oslo bekam sie das Kräglein aus Pelz,
Hoffentlich gefällts, das Kräglein aus Pelz!
Das bekam sie aus Oslo am Sund.

Und was bekam des Soldaten Weib
Aus dem reichen Amsterdam?
Aus Amsterdam bekam sie den Hut
Und er steht ihr gut, der holländische Hut
Den bekam sie aus Amsterdam.

Und was bekam das Soldaten Weib
Aus Brüssel im belgischen Land?
Aus Brüssel bekam sie die seltenen Spitzen!
Ach, das zu besitzen, so seltene Spitzen!
Die bekam sie aus belgischem Land.

Und was bekam des Soldaten Weib
Aus der Lichterstadt Paris?
Aus Paris bekam sie das seidene Kleid,
Zu der Nachbarin Neid das seidene Kleid
Das bekam sie aus Paris.

Und was bekam des Soldaten Weib
Aus dem südlichen Bukarest?
Aus Bukarest bekam sie das Hemd
So bunt und so fremd, ein rumänisches Hemd
Das bekam sie aus Bukarest.

WHAT DID THE SOLDIER'S WIFE RECEIVE?

And what did the soldier's wife receive
From the ancient capital, Prague?
From Prague she received her high-heeled shoes,
Greetings, good news, and her high-heeled shoes
She received from the capital, Prague.

And what did the soldier's wife receive
From Oslo beyond the sound?
She received from Oslo a little fur piece,
And the hope it might please, a little fur piece
She received from beyond the sound.

And what did the soldier's wife receive
From wealthy Amsterdam?
From Amsterdam she received a hat,
She looked well in that, the pretty Dutch hat
She received from Amsterdam.

And what did the soldier's wife receive
From Brussels, the Belgian town?
She received from Brussels the rarest of lace,
What a joy to possess the rarest of lace
She received from the Belgian town.

And what did the soldier's wife receive
From Paris the city of light?
She received from Paris a silken gown,
'Twas the talk of the town, the silken gown
She received from the city of light.

And what did the soldier's wife receive
From the south, from Bucharest?
From Bucharest she received a smock,
A strange gay frock, the Rumanian smock
She received from Bucharest.

Und was bekam des Soldaten Weib
Aus dem weiten Russenland?
Aus Russland bekam sie den Witwenschleier,
Zu der Totenfeir den Witwenschleier
Das bekam sie aus Russenland.

And what did the soldier's wife receive
From the Russian land of snow?
She received from Russia her widow's weeds,
For her grief she had need of those widow's weeds
She received from the land of snow.

DIE MASKE DES BÖSEN

An meiner Wand hängt ein japanisches Holzwerk,
Maske eines bösen Dämons, bemalt mit Goldlack.
Mitfühlend sehe ich
Die geschwollenen Stirnadern, andeutend
Wie anstrengend es ist, böse zu sein.

THE MASK OF EVIL

On my wall hangs a Japanese carving,
The mask of an evil demon, decorated with gold lacquer.
Sympathetically I observe
The swollen veins of the forehead, indicating
What a strain it is to be evil.

GEDANKEN ÜBER DIE DAUER
DES EXILS

1.

Schlage keinen Nagel in die Wand
Wirf den Rock auf den Stuhl!
Warum für vier Tage vorsorgen?
Du kehrst morgen zurück!

Lass den kleinen Baum ohne Wasser!
Wozu einen Baum pflanzen?
Bevor er so hoch wie ein Stufe ist
Gehst du froh weg von hier!

Ziehe die Mütze ins Gesicht, wenn die Leute vorbeikommen!
Wozu in einer fremden Grammatik blättern?
Die Nachricht, die dich heimruft
Ist in bekannter Sprache geschrieben.

So wie der Kalk vom Gebälk blättert
(Tue nichts dagegen!)
Wird der Zaun der Gewalt zermorschen
Der an der Grenze aufgerichtet ist
Gegen die Gerechtigkeit.

2.

Sieh den Nagel in der Wand, den du eingeschlagen hast!
Wann, glaubst du, wirst du zurückkehren?
Willst du wissen, was du im Innersten glaubst?

Tag um Tag
Arbeitest du an der Befreiung,
Sitzend in der Kammer schreibst du,
Willst du wissen, was du von deiner Arbeit hältst?
Sieh den kleinen Kastanienbaum im Eck des Hofes
Zu dem du die Kanne voll Wasser schlepptest!

THOUGHTS CONCERNING THE DURATION OF EXILE

1.

Don't drive a nail into the wall,
Throw your coat on a chair!
Why bother about four days?
Tomorrow you'll go back.

Let the little tree go unwatered!
Why plant a tree at all?
Before it's as high as a stair tread
You'll be happily leaving this place.

Pull your cap over your eyes when you pass people!
Why turn the pages of a strange grammar?
The news that calls you home
Is written in a familiar language.

As the calcimine peels from the roofbeam
(Do nothing to stop it)
So the fence of force will crumble
That has been reared up on the border
Against justice.

2.

See the nail in the wall, the nail you hammered into it!
When do you think you'll be going back?
Do you want to know what you really believe in your heart?

Day after day
You work for the liberation,
Sitting in your room writing.
Do you want to know what you really think of your work?
Look at the little chestnut tree in the corner of the courtyard
That you carry your canful of water to.

DIE LANDSCHAFT DES EXILS

Aber auch ich, auf dem letzten Boot,
Sah noch den Frohsinn des Frührots im Takelzeug
Und der Delphine grauliche Leiber tauchen
Aus der Japanischen See.

Die Pferdewäglein mit dem Goldbeschlag
Und die rosa Armschleier der Matronen
In den Gassen des gezeichneten Manila
Sah auch der Flüchtende mit Freude.

Die Öltürme und dürstenden Gärten von Los Angeles
Und die abendlichen Schluchten Kaliforniens und die Obstmärkte
Liessen auch den Boten des Unglücks
Nicht kalt.

LANDSCAPE OF EXILE

But even I, on the last boat,
Saw the gaiety of dawn in the rigging
And the grayish bodies of dolphins emerge
From the Japanese Sea

The little horsecarts with gilt decorations
And the pink sleeves of the matrons
In the alleys of doomed Manila
The fugitive beheld with joy.

The oil derricks and the thirsty gardens of Los Angeles
And the ravines of California at evening and the fruit market
Did not leave the messenger of misfortune unmoved.

DIE RÜCKKEHR

Die Vaterstadt, wie find ich sie doch?
Folgend den Bomberschwärmen
Komm ich nach Haus.
Wo denn liegt sie? Wo die ungeheuren
Gebirge von Rauch stehn.
Das in den Feuern dort
Ist sie.

Die Vaterstadt, wie empfängt sie mich wohl?
Vor mir kommen die Bomber. Tödliche Schwärme
Melden euch meine Rückkehr. Feuersbrünste
Gehen dem Sohn voraus.

THE RETURN

The city of my fathers, how can I find it?
Following the swarms of bombers
I come home.
Where does it lie? Yonder where huge
Mountains of smoke arise.
There in the flames
It stands.

The city of my fathers, how shall it receive me?
The bombers arrive before me. Deadly swarms
Announce my approach. Conflagrations
Precede the son's return.

AN DIE NACHGEBORENEN

1.

Wirklich, ich lebe in finsteren Zeiten!
Das arglose Wort ist töricht. Eine glatte Stirn
Deutet auf Unempfindlichkeit hin. Der Lachende
Hat die furchtbare Nachricht
Nur noch nicht empfangen.

Was sind das für Zeiten, wo
Ein Gespräch über Bäume fast ein Verbrechen ist
Weil es ein Schweigen über so viele Untaten einschliesst!
Der dort ruhig über die Strasse geht
Ist wohl nicht mehr erreichbar für seine Freunde
Die in Not sind?

Es ist wahr: ich verdiene noch meinen Unterhalt
Aber glaubt mir: das ist nur ein Zufall. Nichts
Von dem, was ich tue, berechtigt mich dazu, mich sattzuessen.
Zufällig bin ich verschont. (Wenn mein Glück aussetzt
Bin ich verloren.)

Man sagt mir: iss und trink du! Sei froh, dass du hast!
Aber wie kann ich essen und trinken, wenn
Ich es dem Hungerenden entreisse, was ich esse, und
Mein Glas Wasser einem Verdurstenden fehlt?
Und doch esse und trinke ich.

Ich wäre gerne weise.
In den altern Büchern steht, was weise ist:
Sich aus dem Streit der Welt halten und die kurze Zeit
Ohne Furcht verbringen
Auch ohne Gewalt auskommen
Böses mit Gutem vergelten
Seine Wünsche nicht erfüllen, sondern vergessen
Gilt für weise.
Alles das kann ich nicht:
Wirklich, ich lebe in finsteren Zeiten!

TO POSTERITY

1.

Indeed I live in the dark ages!
A guileless word is an absurdity. A smooth forehead betokens
A hard heart. He who laughs
Has not yet heard
The terrible tidings.

Ah, what an age it is
When to speak of trees is almost a crime
For it is a kind of silence about injustice!
And he who walks calmly across the street,
Is he not out of reach of his friends
In trouble?

It is true: I earn my living
But, believe me, it is only an accident.
Nothing that I do entitles me to eat my fill.
By chance I was spared. (If my luck leaves me
I am lost.)

They tell me: eat and drink. Be glad you have it!
But how can I eat and drink
When my food is snatched from the hungry
And my glass of water belongs to the thirsty?
And yet I eat and drink.

I would gladly be wise.
The old books tell us what wisdom is:
Avoid the strife of the world, live out your little time
Fearing no one,
Using no violence,
Returning good for evil—
Not fulfillment of desire but forgetfulness
Passes for wisdom.
I can do none of this:
Indeed I live in the dark ages!

2.

In die Städte kam ich zu der Zeit der Unordnung
Als da Hunger herrschte.
Unter die Menschen kam ich zu der Zeit des Aufruhrs
Und ich empörte mich mit ihnen.
So verging meine Zeit
Die auf Erden mir gegeben war.

Mein Essen ass ich zwischen den Schlachten.
Schlafen legte ich mich unter die Mörder.
Der Liebe pflegte ich achtlos
Und die Natur sah ich ohne Geduld.
So verging meine Zeit
Die auf Erden mir gegeben war.

Die Strassen führten in den Sumpf zu meiner Zeit.
Die Sprache verriet mich dem Schlächter.
Ich vermochte nur wenig. Aber die Herrschenden
Sassen ohne mich sicherer, das hoffte ich.
So verging meine Zeit
Die auf Erden mir gegeben war.

Die Kräfte waren gering. Das Ziel
Lag in grosser Ferne,
Es war deutlich sichtbar, wenn auch für mich
Kaum zu erreichen.
So verging meine Zeit
Die auf Erden mir gegeben war.

3.

Ihr, die ihr auftauchen werdet aus der Flut
In der wir untergegangen sind,
Gedenkt
Wenn ihr von unsern Schwächen sprecht
Auch der finsteren Zeit
Der ihr entronnen seid.

I came to the cities in a time of disorder
When hunger ruled.
I came among men in a time of uprising
And I revolted with them.
So the time passed away
Which on earth was given me.

I ate my food between massacres.
The shadow of murder lay upon my sleep.
And when I loved, I loved with indifference.
I looked upon nature with impatience.
So the time passed away
Which on earth was given me.

In my time streets led to the quicksand.
Speech betrayed me to the slaughterer.
There was little I could do. But without me
The rulers would have been more secure. This was my hope.
So the time passed away
Which on earth was given me.

Men's strength was little. The goal
Lay far in the distance,
Easy to see if for me
Scarcely attainable.
So the time passed away
Which on earth was given me.

3.

You, who shall emerge from the flood
In which we are sinking,
Think—
When you speak of our weaknesses,
Also of the dark time
That brought them forth.

Gingen wir doch, öfter als die Schuhe die Länder wechselnd
Durch die Kriege der Klassen, verzweifelt
Wenn da nur Unrecht war und keine Empörung.

Dabei wissen wir ja:
Auch der Hass gegen die Niedrigkeit
Verzerrt die Züge.
Auch der Zorn über das Unrecht
Macht die Stimme heiser. Ach, wir
Die wir den Boden bereiten wollten für Freundlichkeit
Konnten selber nicht freundlich sein.

Ihr aber, wenn es so weit sein wird
Dass der Mensch dem Mensch ein Helfer ist,
Gedenkt unsrer
Mit Nachsicht.

For we went, changing our country more often than our shoes,
In the class war, despairing
When there was only injustice and no resistance.

For we knew only too well:
Even the hatred of squalor
Makes the brow grow stern.
Even anger against injustice
Makes the voice grow harsh. Alas, we
Who wished to lay the foundations of kindness
Could not ourselves be kind.

But you, when at last it comes to pass
That man can help his fellow man,
Do not judge us
Too harshly.

KINDERLIEDER, ULM 1592

Bischof, ich kann fliegen
Sagte der Schneider zum Bischof.
Pass auf, wie ich's mach!
Und er stieg mit so 'nen Dingen
Die aussahn wie Schwingen
Auf das grosse, grosse Kirchendach.
Der Bischof ging weiter.
Das sind lauter so Lügen
Der Mensch ist kein Vogel
Es wird nie ein Mensch fliegen
Sagte der Bischof vom Schneider.

Der Schneider ist verschieden
Sagten die Leute dem Bischof.
Es war eine Hatz.
Seine Flügel sind zerspellet
Und er liegt zerschellet
Auf dem harten, harten Kirchenplatz.
Die Glocken sollen läuten
Es waren nichts als Lügen
Der Mensch ist kein Vogel
Es wird nie ein Mensch fliegen
Sagte der Bischof den Leuten.

Bishop, I can fly,
The tailor said to the Bishop.
Just watch how it works.
And he climbed with things
That looked like wings
To the broad, broad roof of the church.
The Bishop passed by.
It's all a lie,
Man is no bird,
No one will ever fly,
The Bishop said of the tailor.

The tailor is done for,
The people said to the Bishop.
It was the talk of the fair.
His wings were smashed
And he was dashed
On the hard, hard stones of the square.
Toll the bells in the steeple,
It was all a lie,
Man is no bird,
No one will ever fly,
The Bishop said to the people.

Distinguished books of poetry available in paperbound

editions from Harcourt Brace Jovanovich, Inc.

James Weldon Johnson, ed.   *The Book of American Negro Poetry*
HPL 43

Ron Loewinsohn   *Meat Air: Poems 1957–1969*
HB 170

Robert Lowell   *Lord Weary's Castle* and *The Mills of the Kavanaughs*
HB 139

Claude McKay   *Selected Poems of Claude McKay*
HB 161

Molière   *The Misanthrope* and *Tartuffe*
HB 96

Tartuffe
HB 130

St.-John Perse   *Anabasis*
H 082

Carl Sandburg   *Harvest Poems: 1910–1960*
HB 36

Honey and Salt
HPL 15

William Shakespeare   *Hamlet*
H 001

King Henry the Fourth, Parts I and II
H 004

Macbeth
H 002

Twelfth Night
H 003

Louis Simpson   *Selected Poems*
HB 29

Sophocles   *The Oedipus Cycle*
HB 8

François Villon   *Poems of François Villon*
H 054

Philip Whalen   *On Bear's Head: Poems 1950–1967*
HB 165

Richard Wilbur   *The Poems of Richard Wilbur*
HB 67